WE ALL NEED MAINTENANCE

Coloring Book

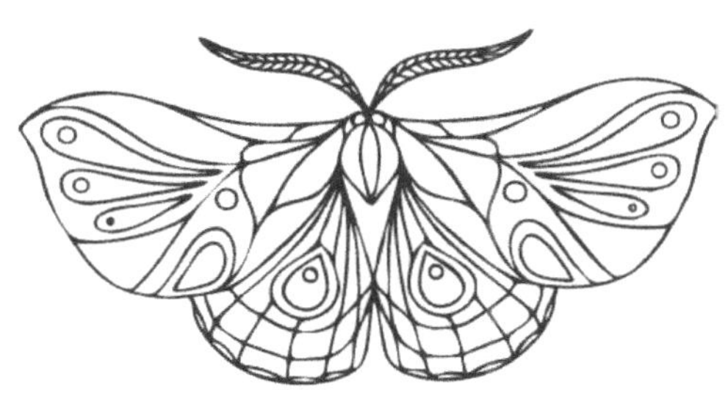

RIA JAY PUBLISHING
ATLANTA GA

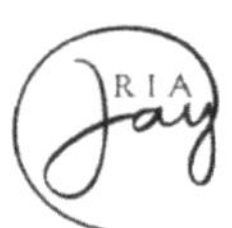

ISBN 978-1-955727-36-5

Published by RIA JAY Publishing
3355 Lenox Road Suite 750 Atlanta, GA 30326
www.riajay.com

Image designs— Canva
Cover design— Bogrodstd, GDJ, Pixabay

Printed in the United States of America First printing January 2023

Acknowledging that we all need maintenance is a beautiful thing!

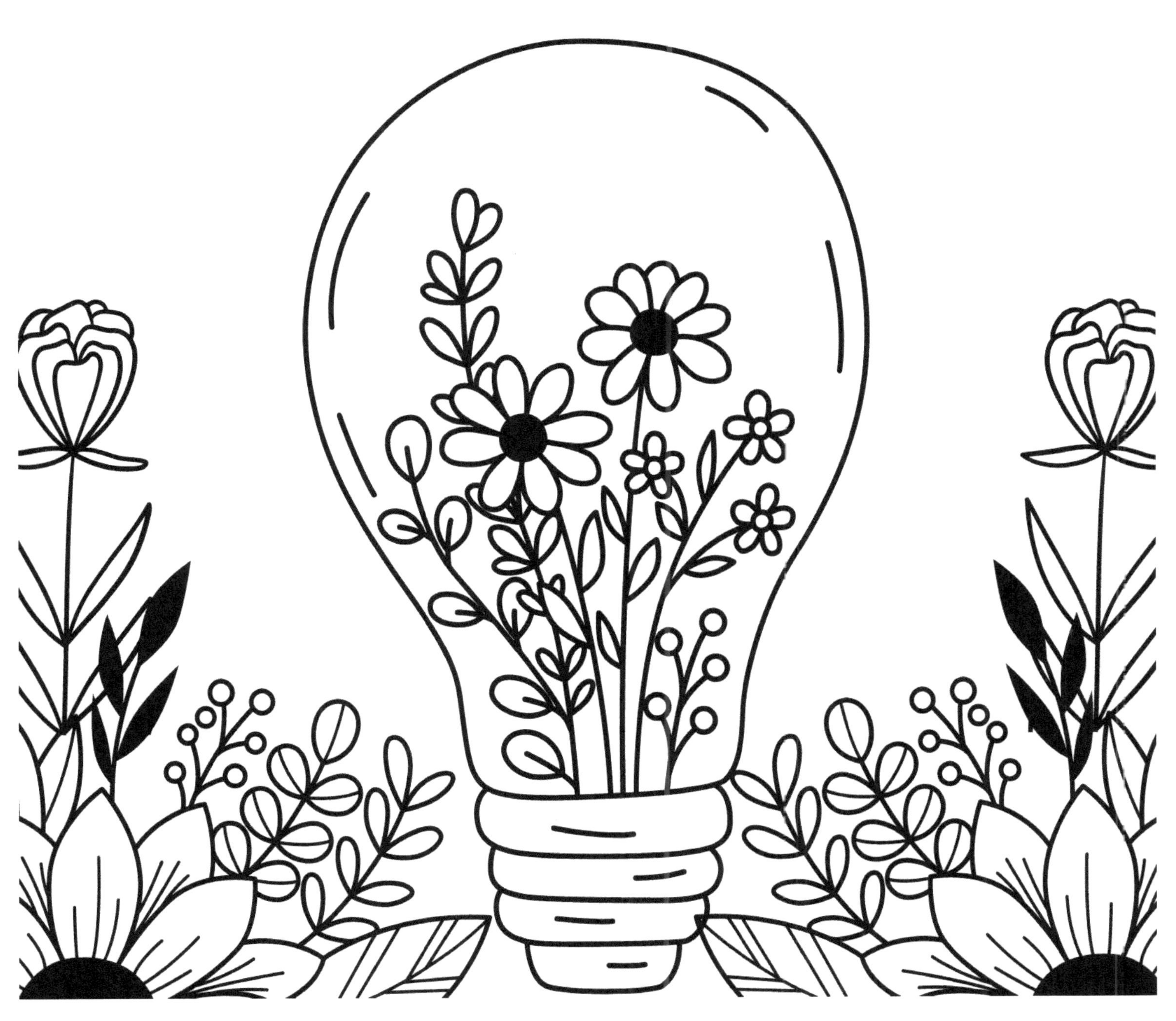

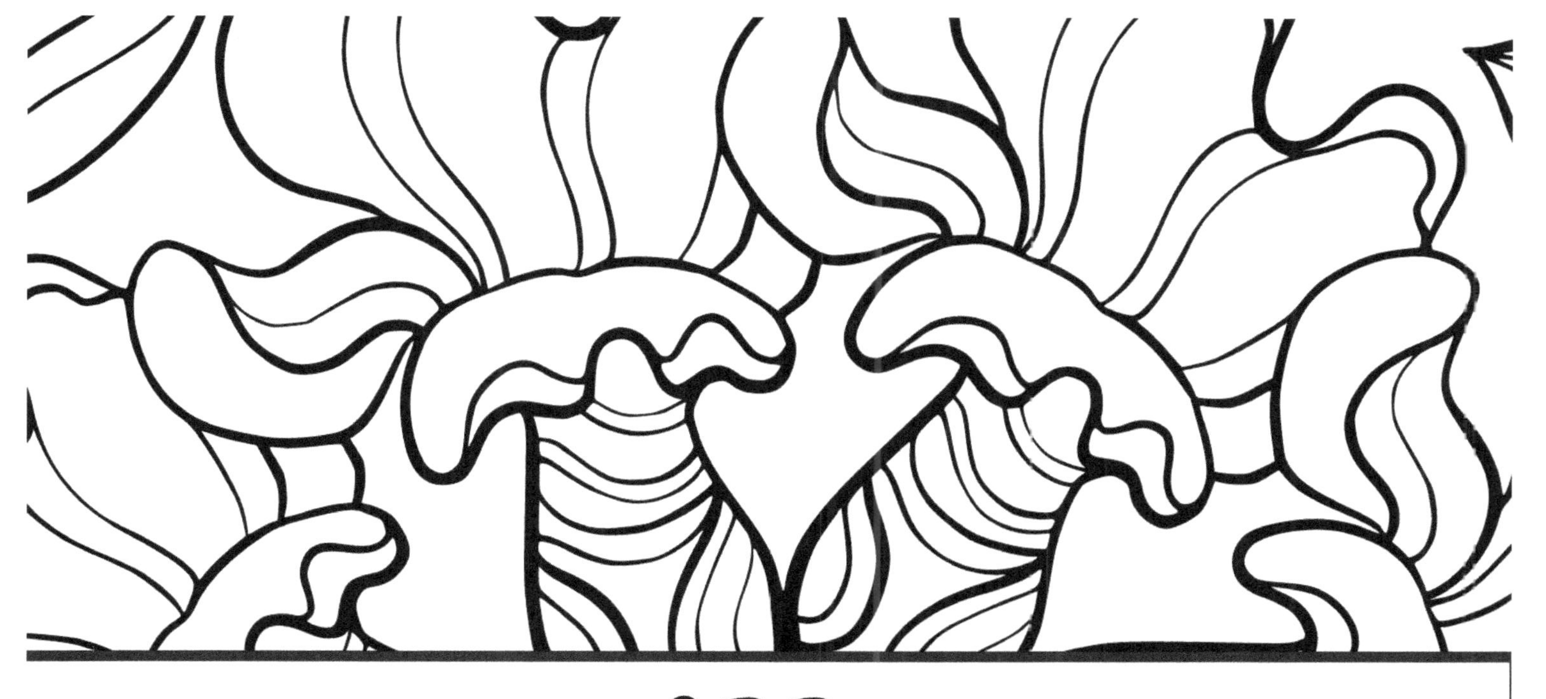

I will not allow my past to define me.

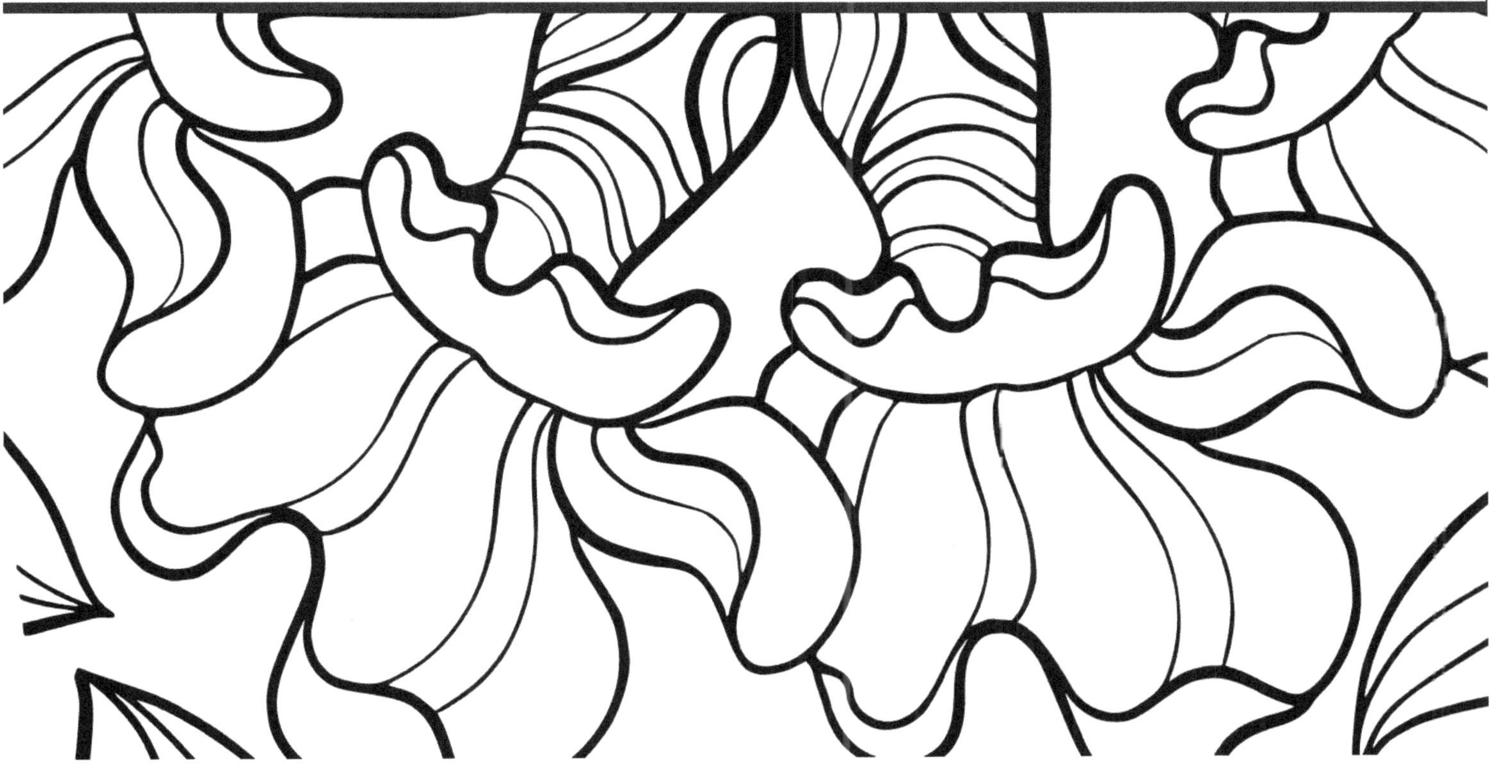

Give yourself flowers often, instead of every blue moon.

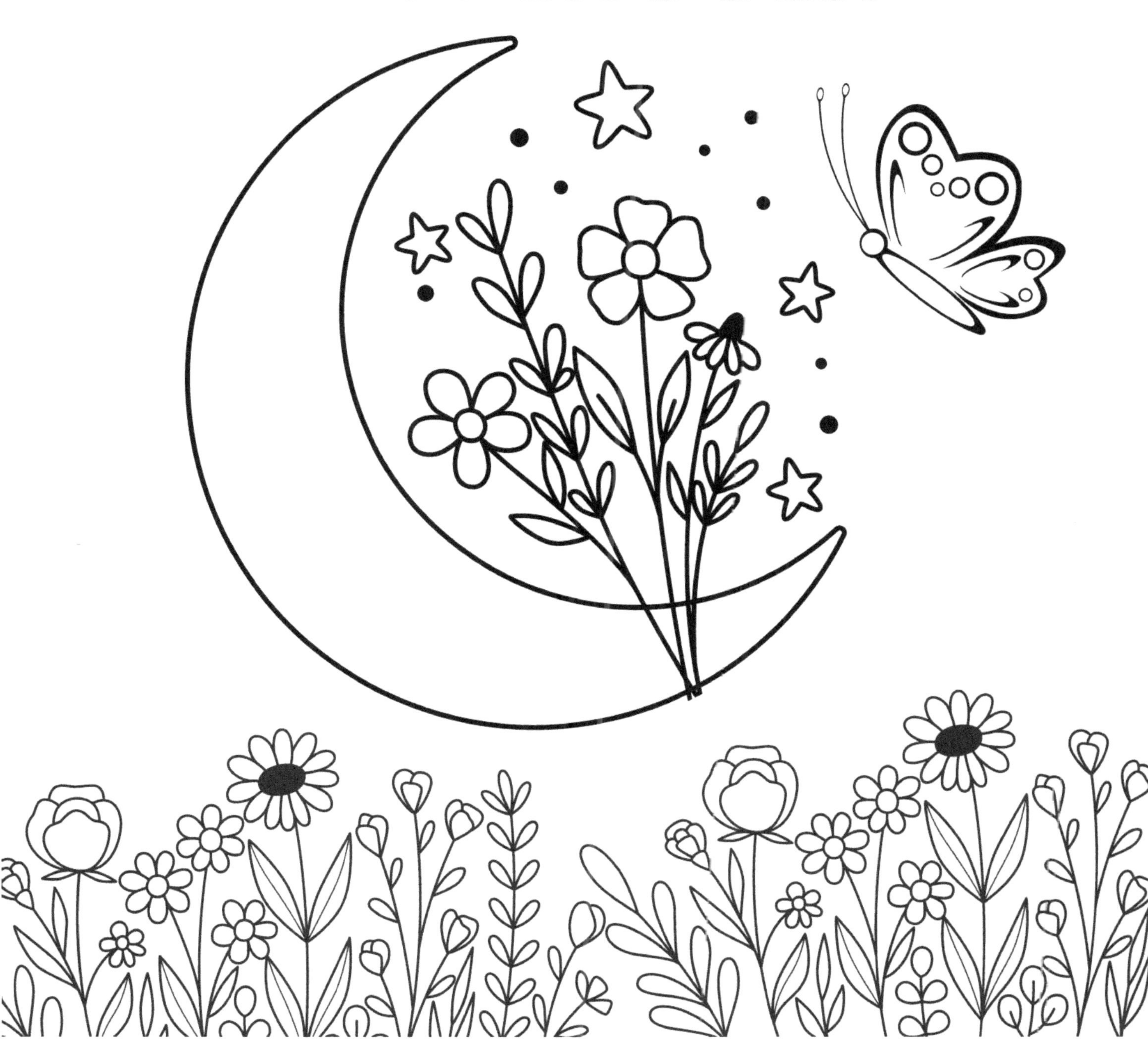

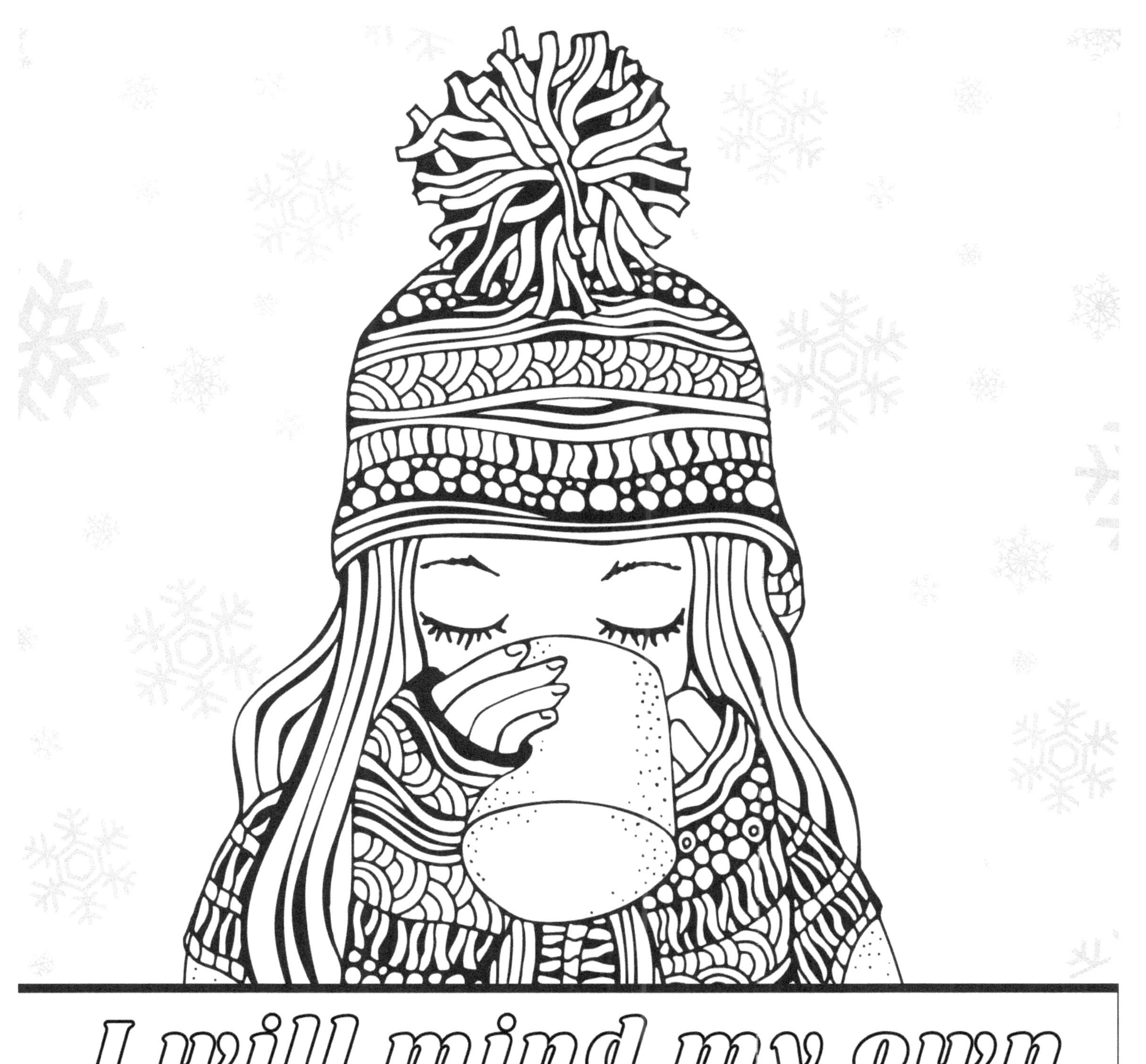

I will mind my own business & work on my mindset.

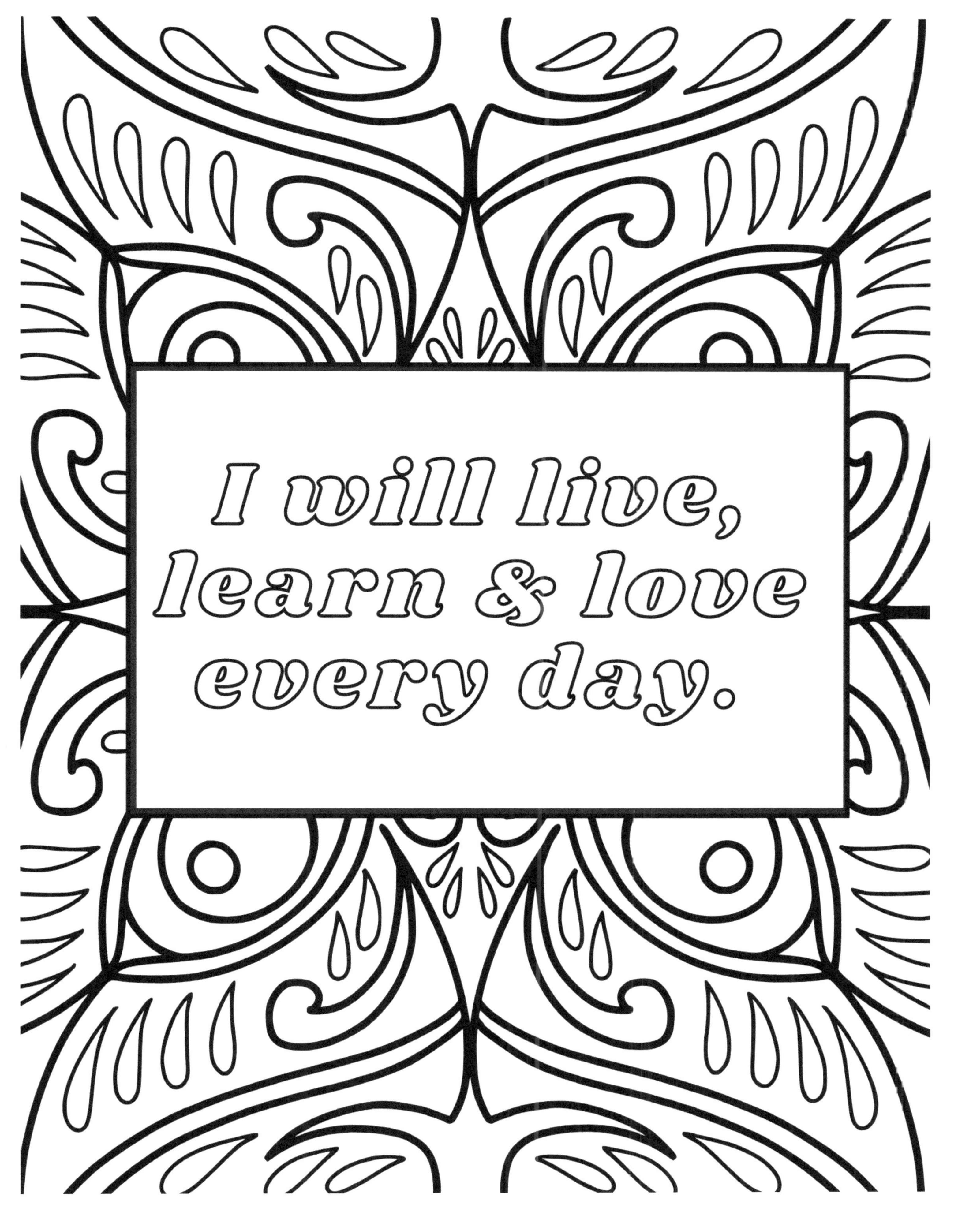
I will live,
learn & love
every day.

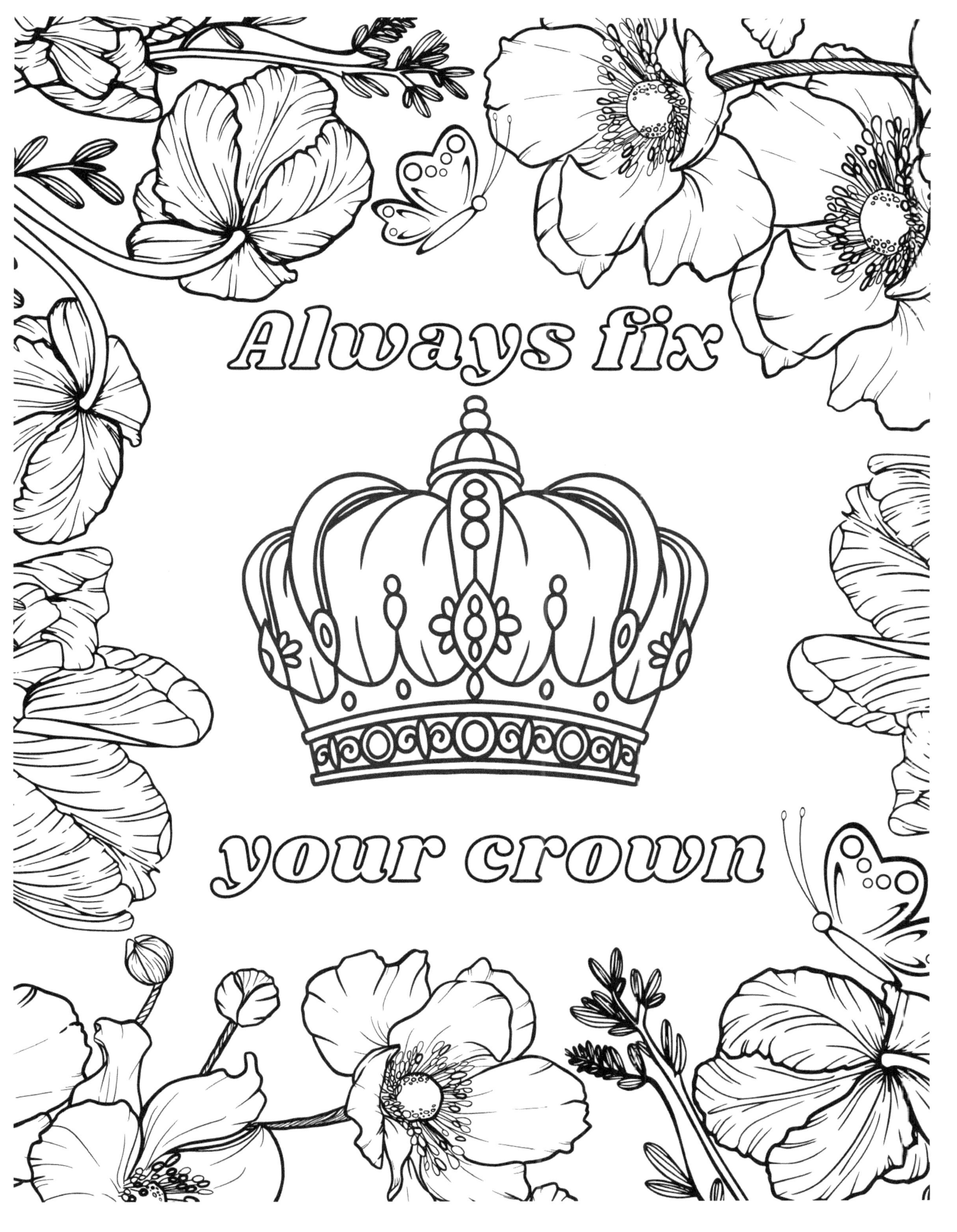
Always fix
your crown

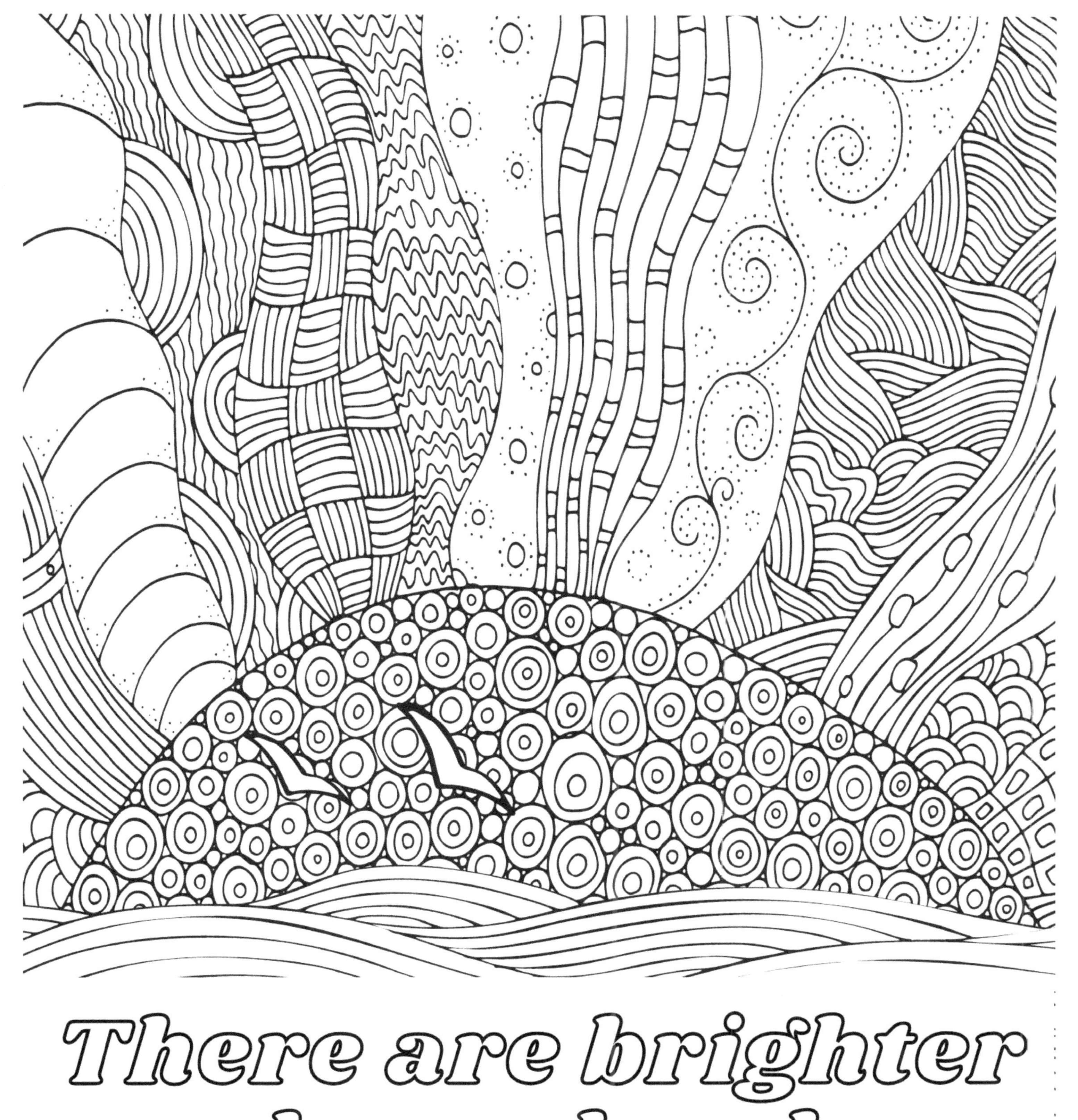

There are brighter days ahead.

There's always sunshine after the rain.

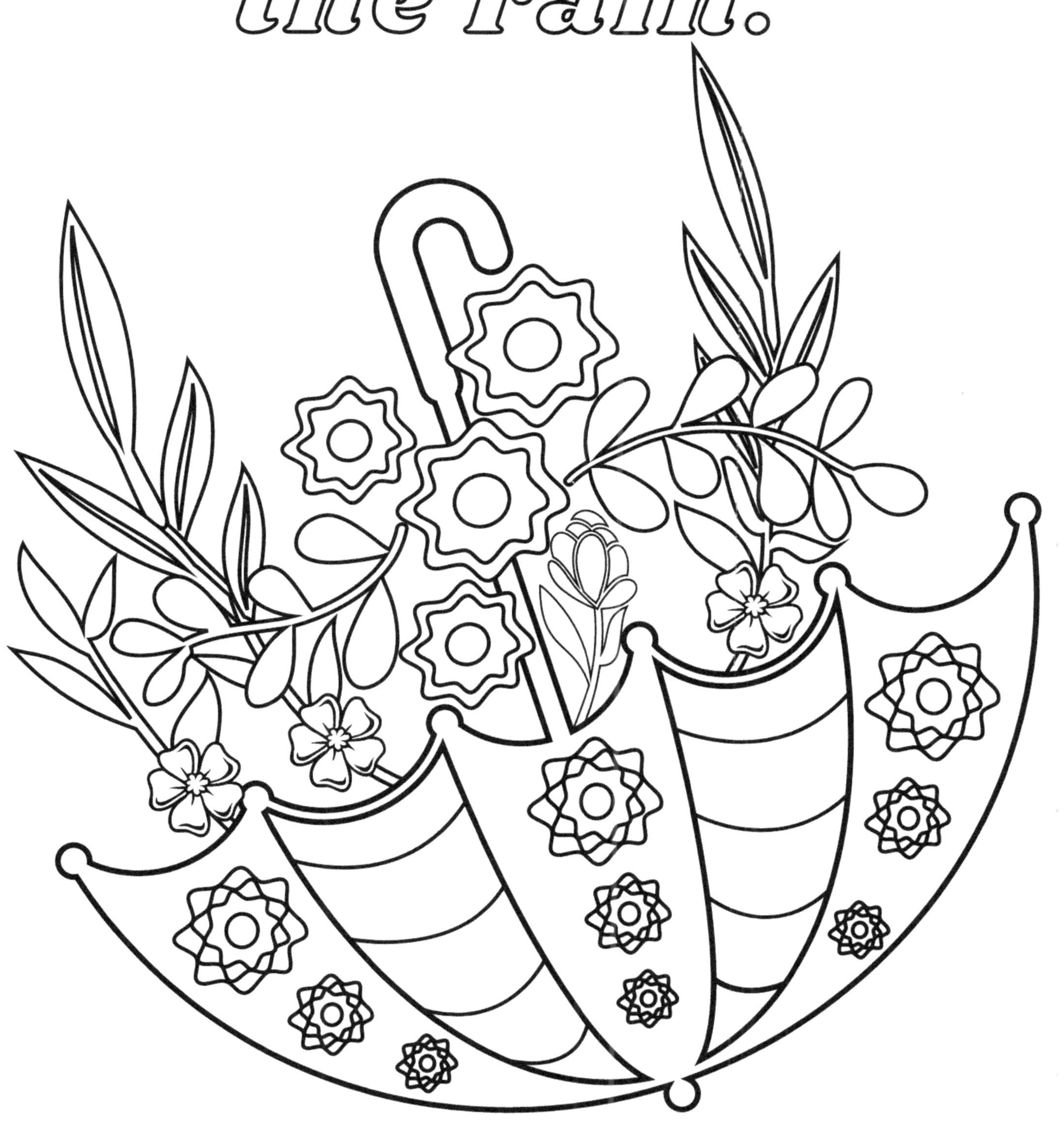

There's always sunshine after the rain.

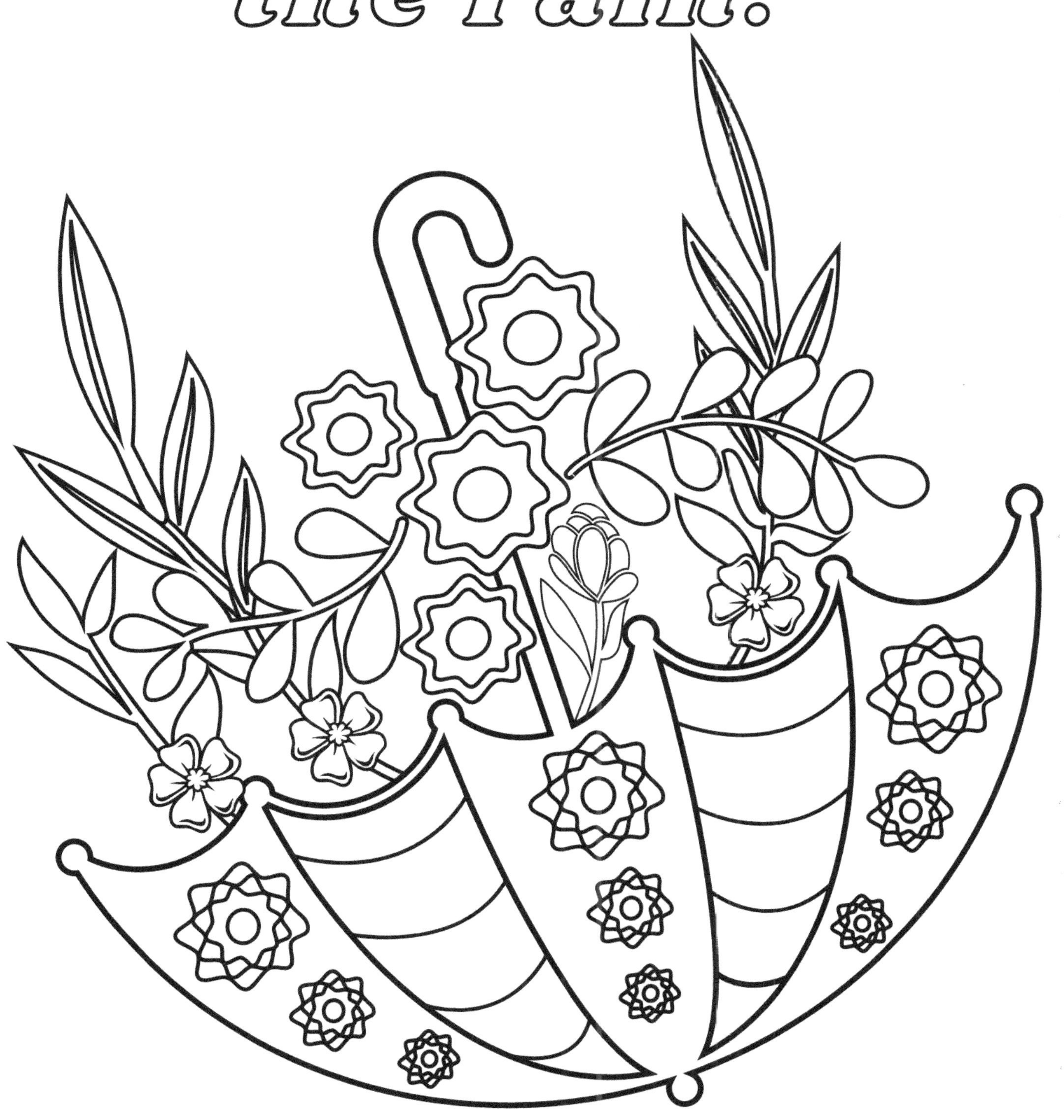

I am grounded.

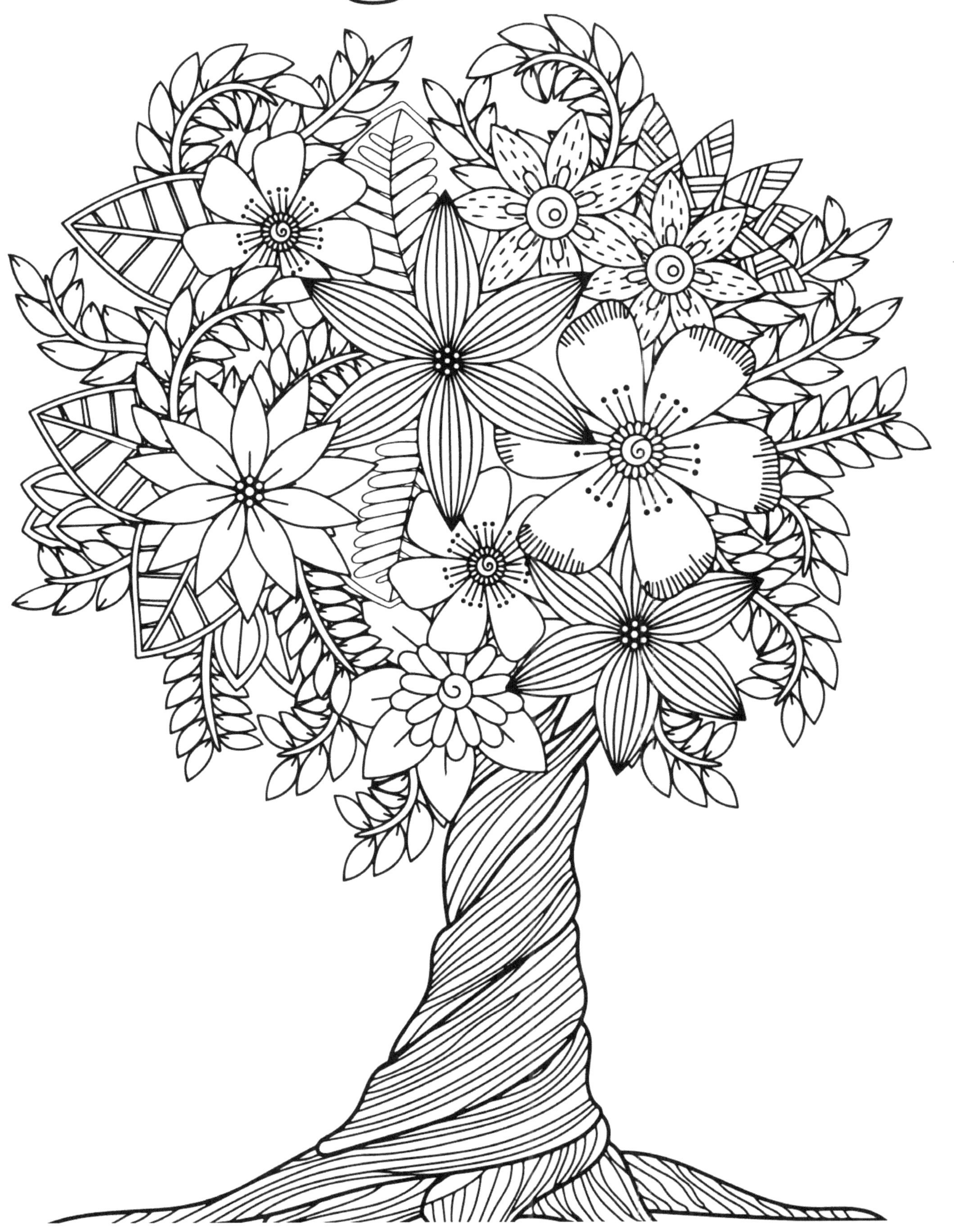

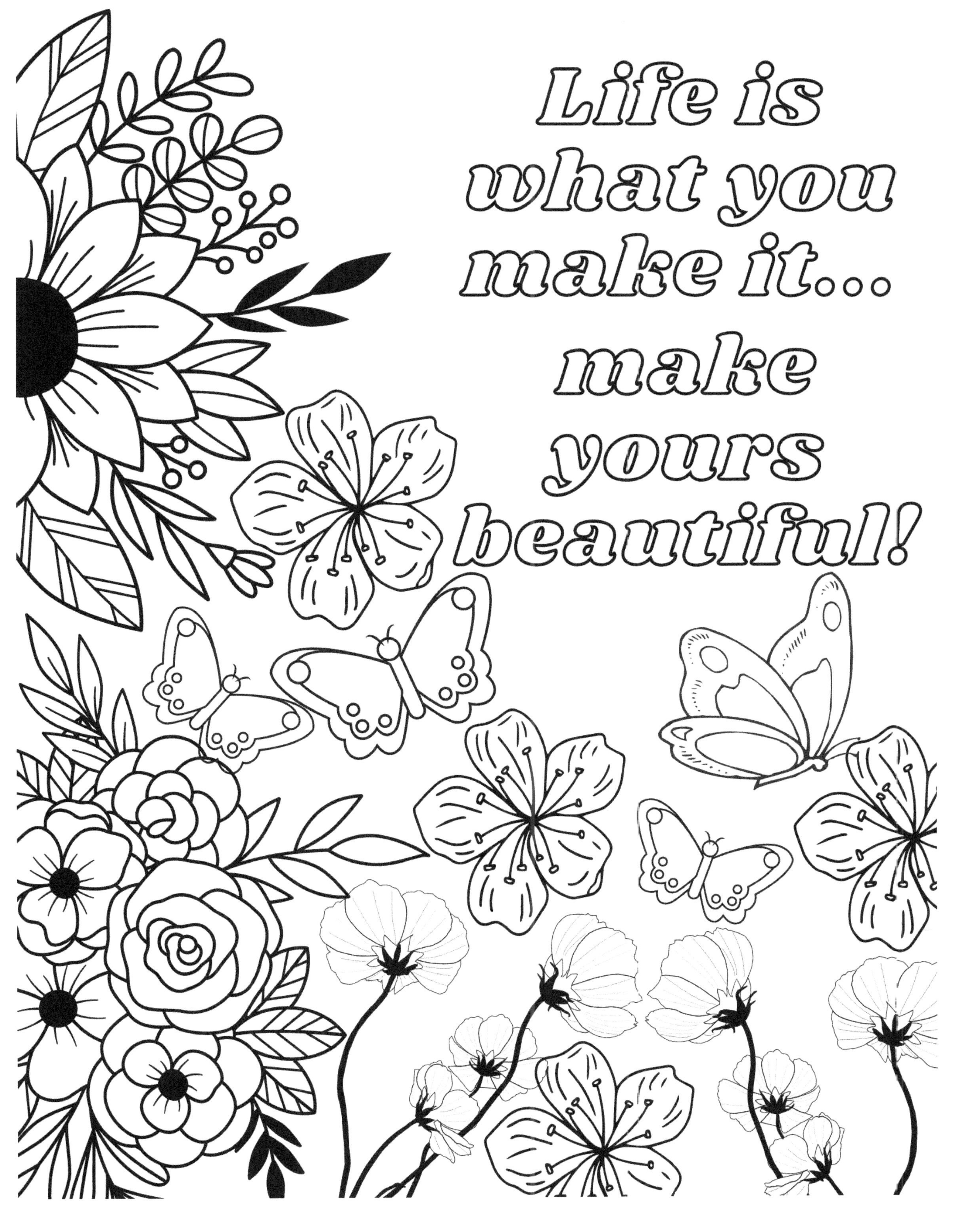
Life is
what you
make it...
make
yours
beautiful!

Grow where you are planted.

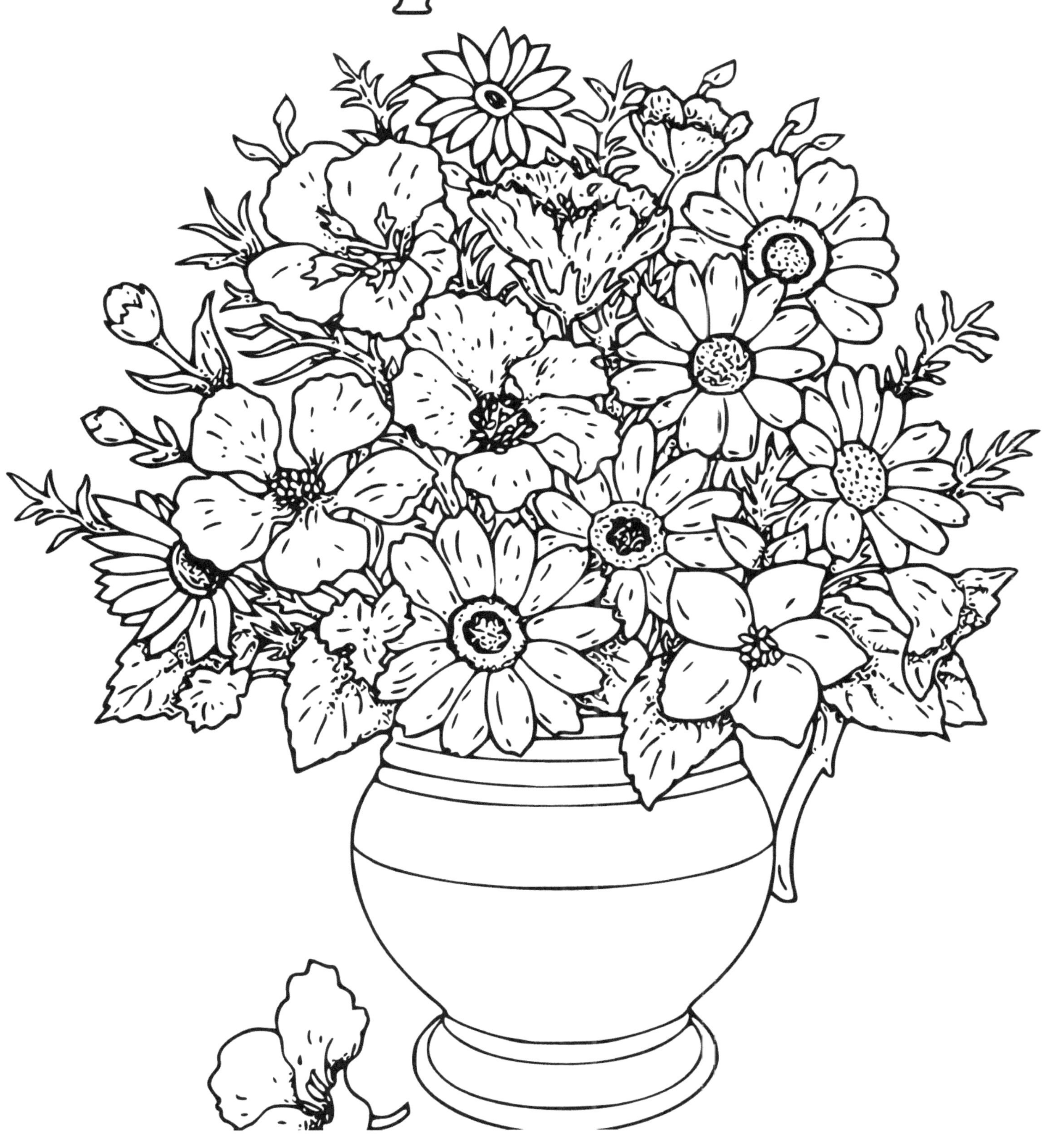

I will water myself daily.

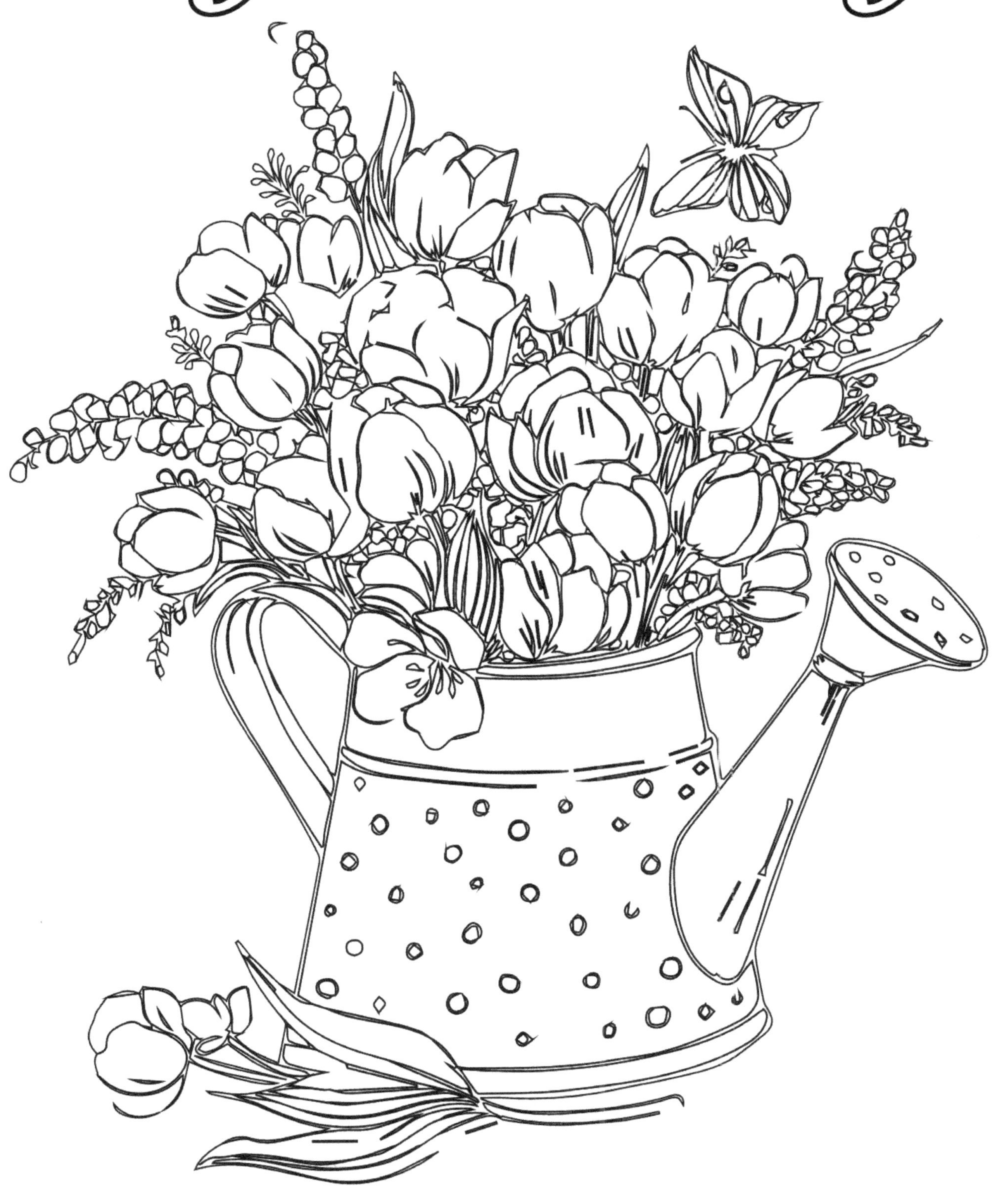

I will confidently strut my stuff!

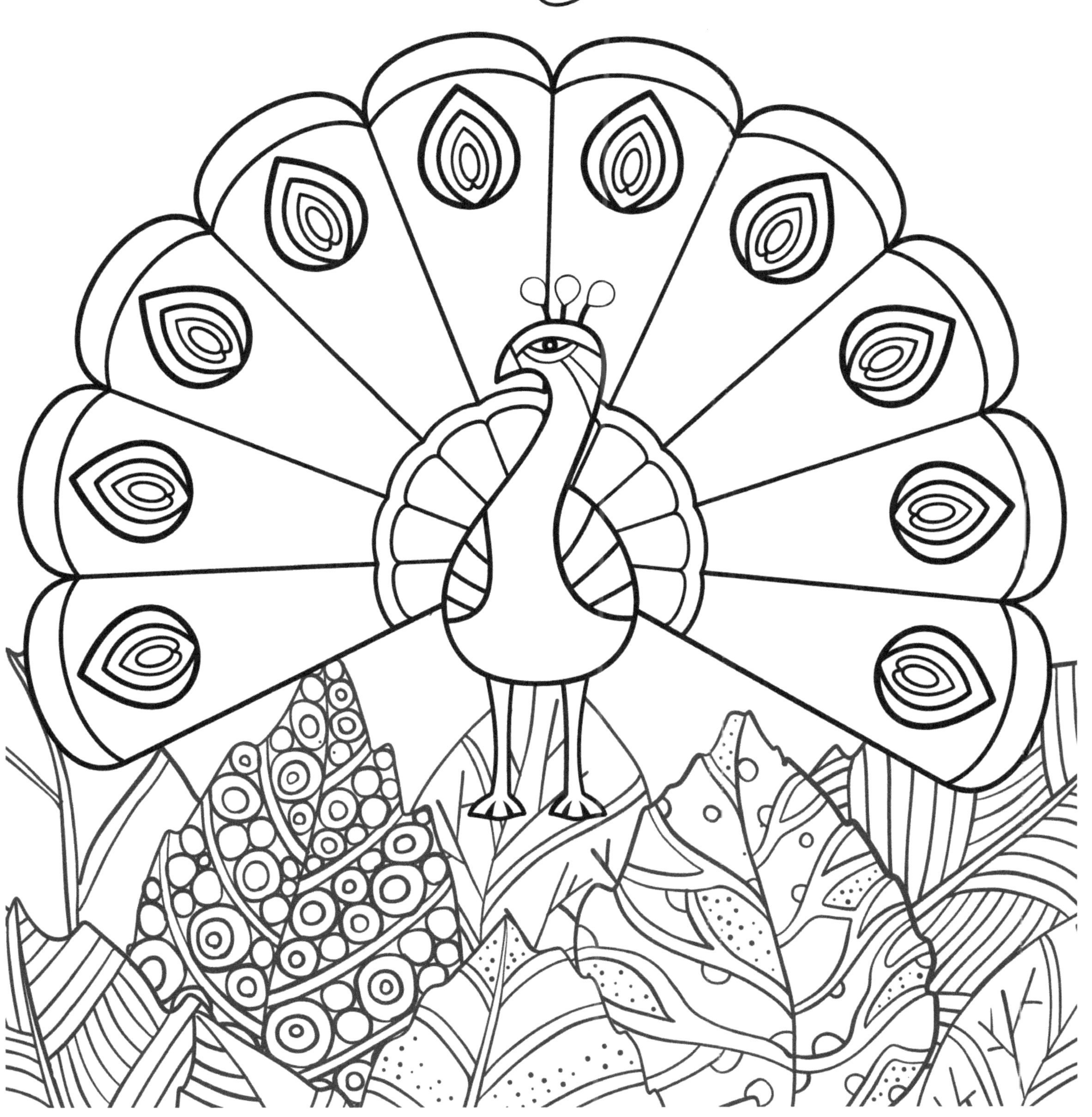

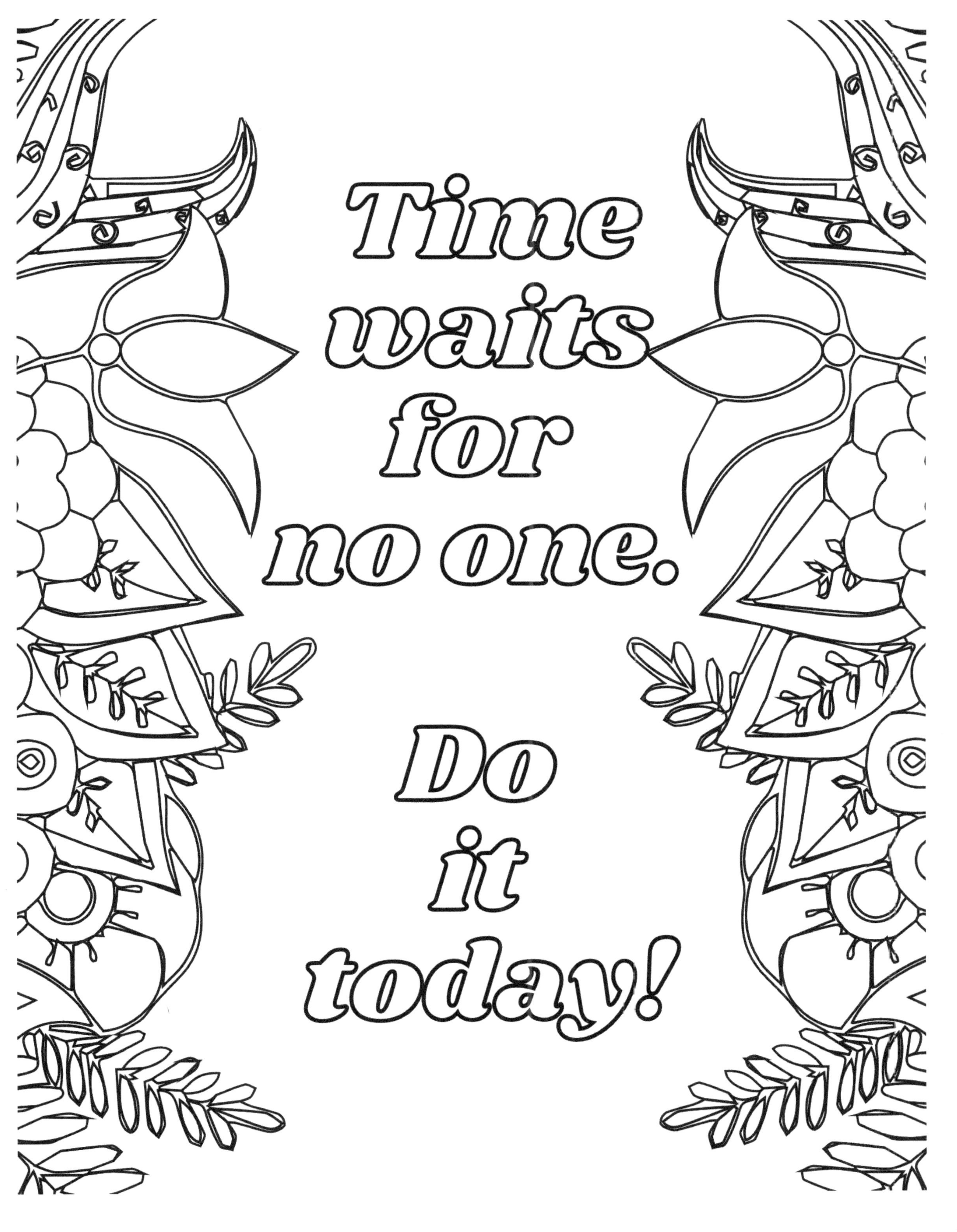
Time waits for no one.
Do it today!

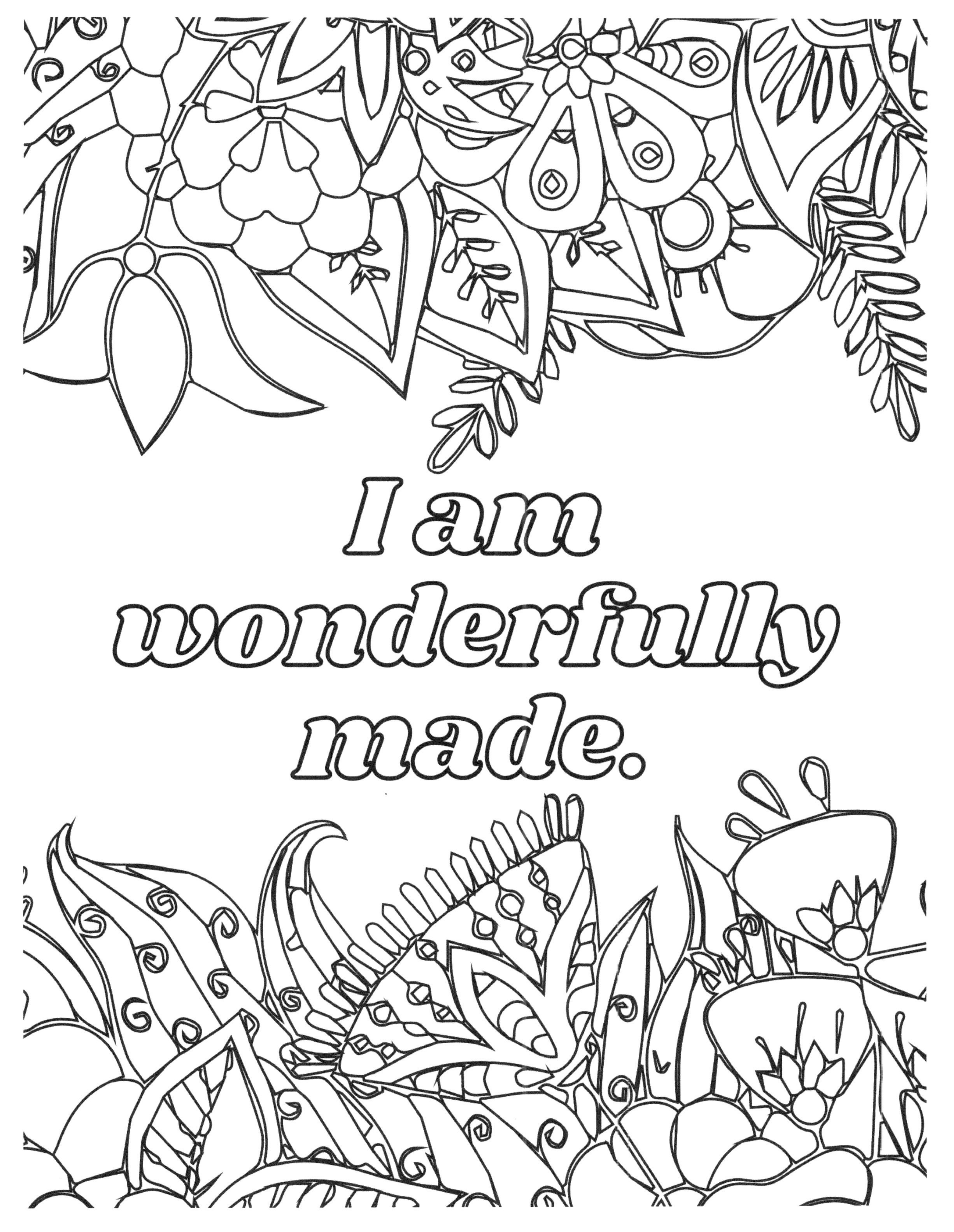
I am
wonderfully
made.

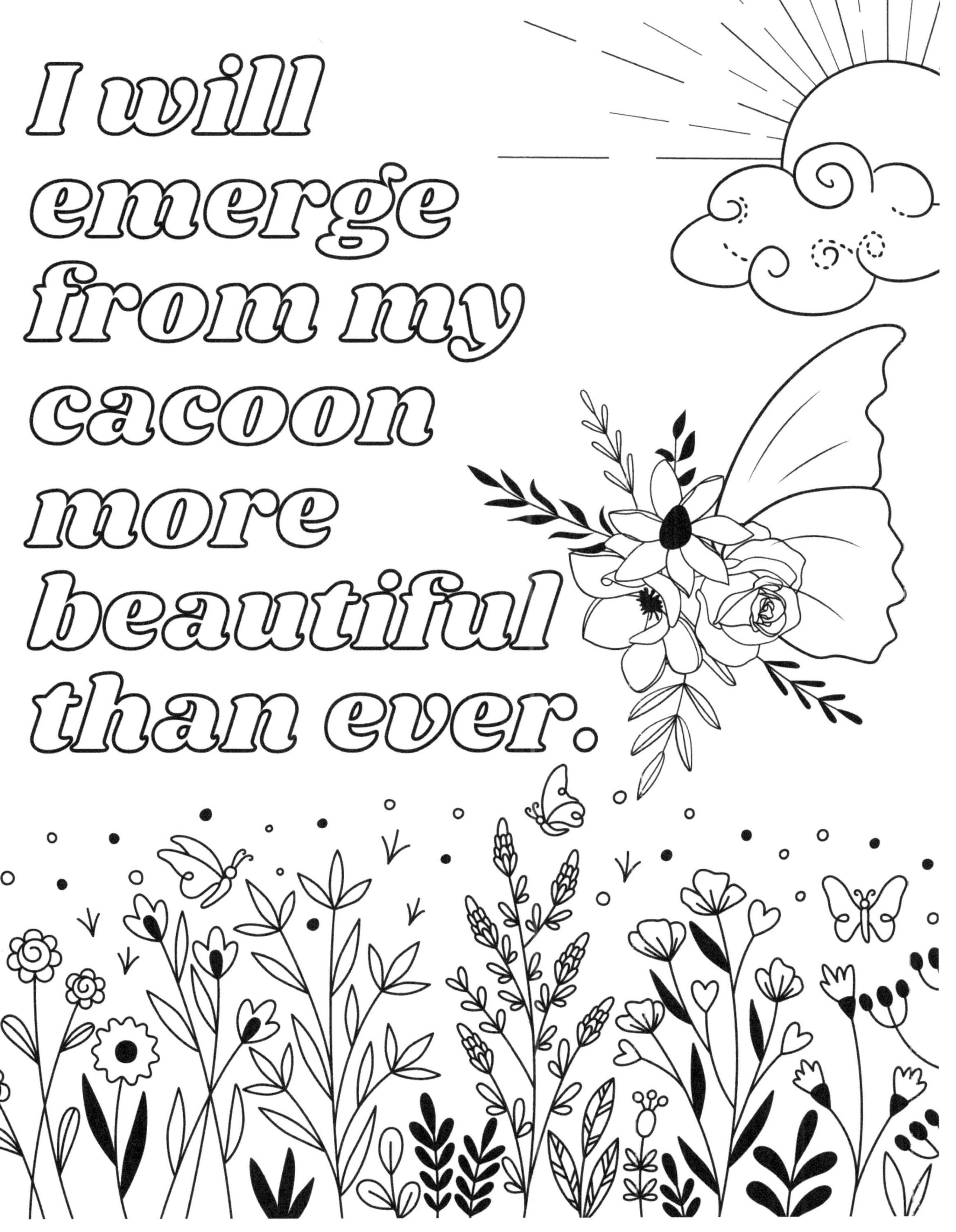
I will emerge from my cacoon more beautiful than ever.

Growth is loving yourself.

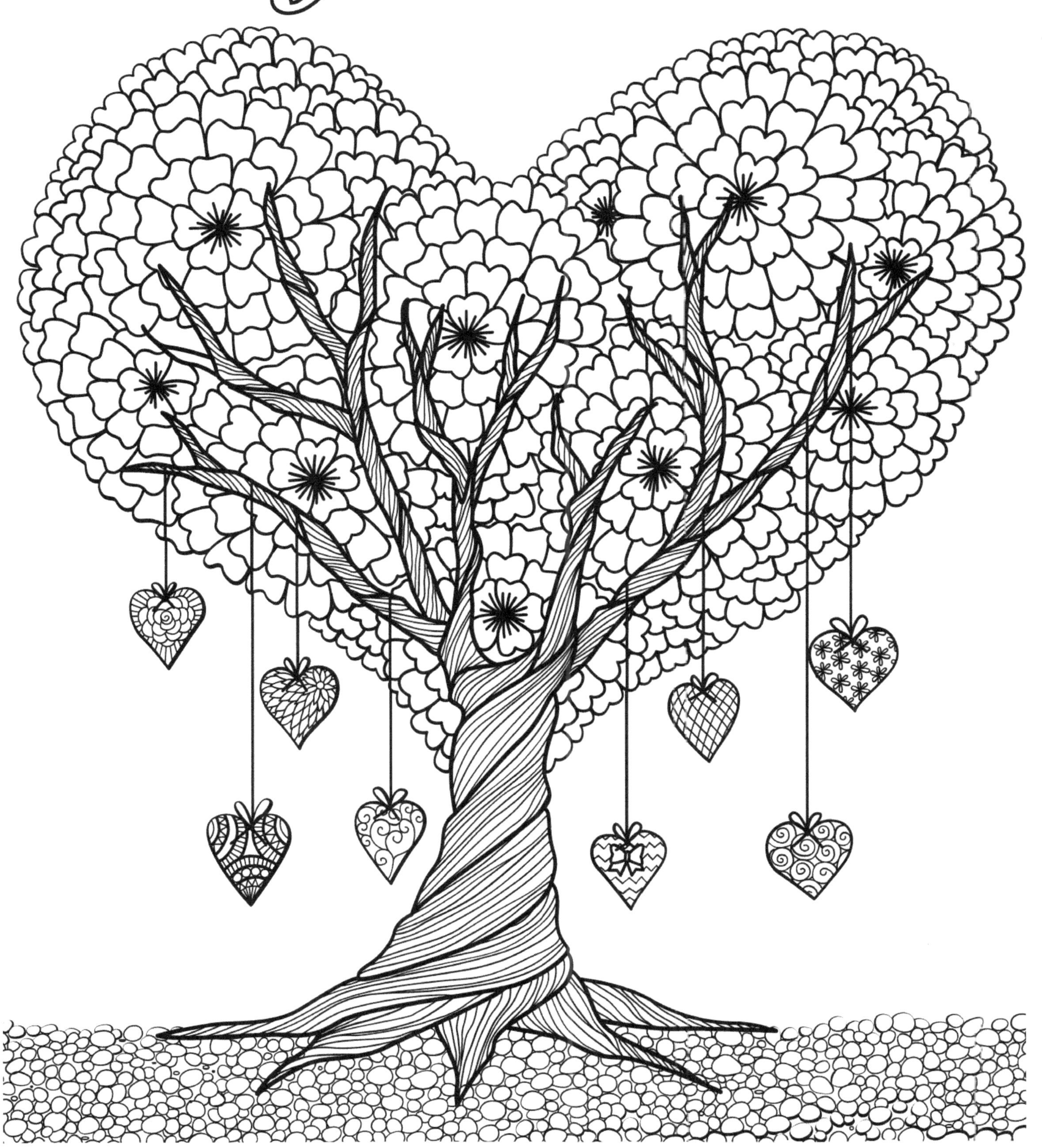

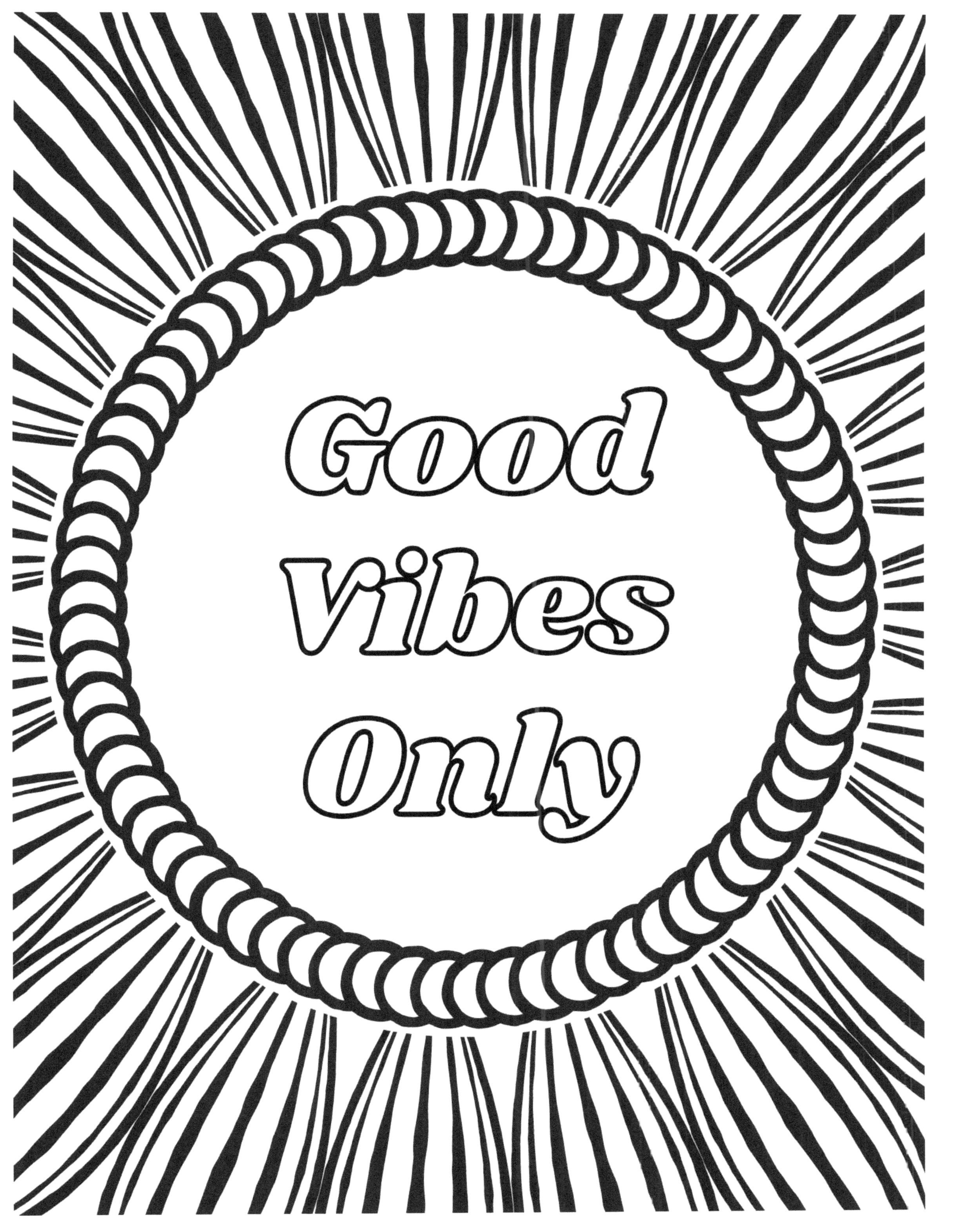
Good
Vibes
Only

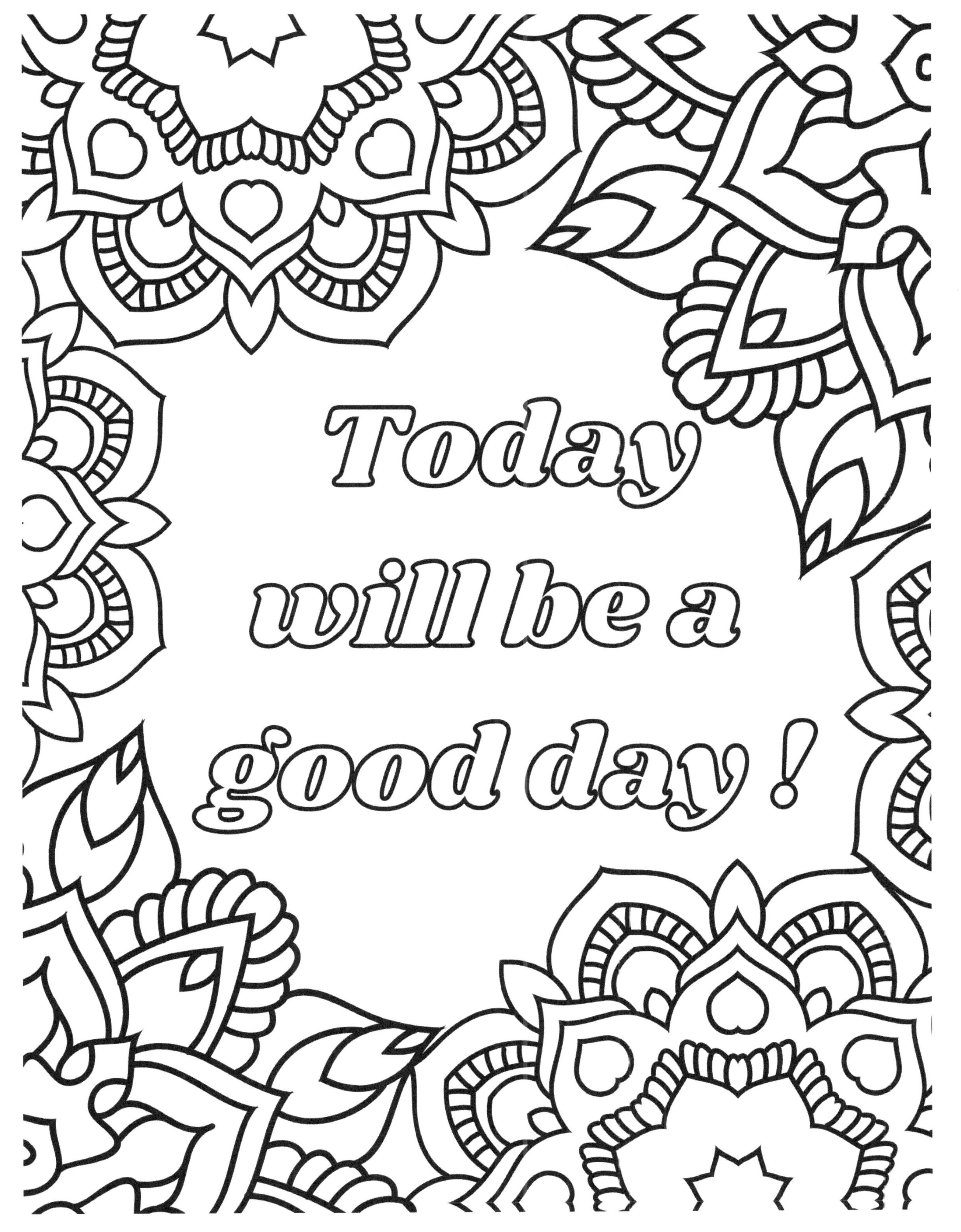
Today
will be a
good day !

I am fierce and fabulous!

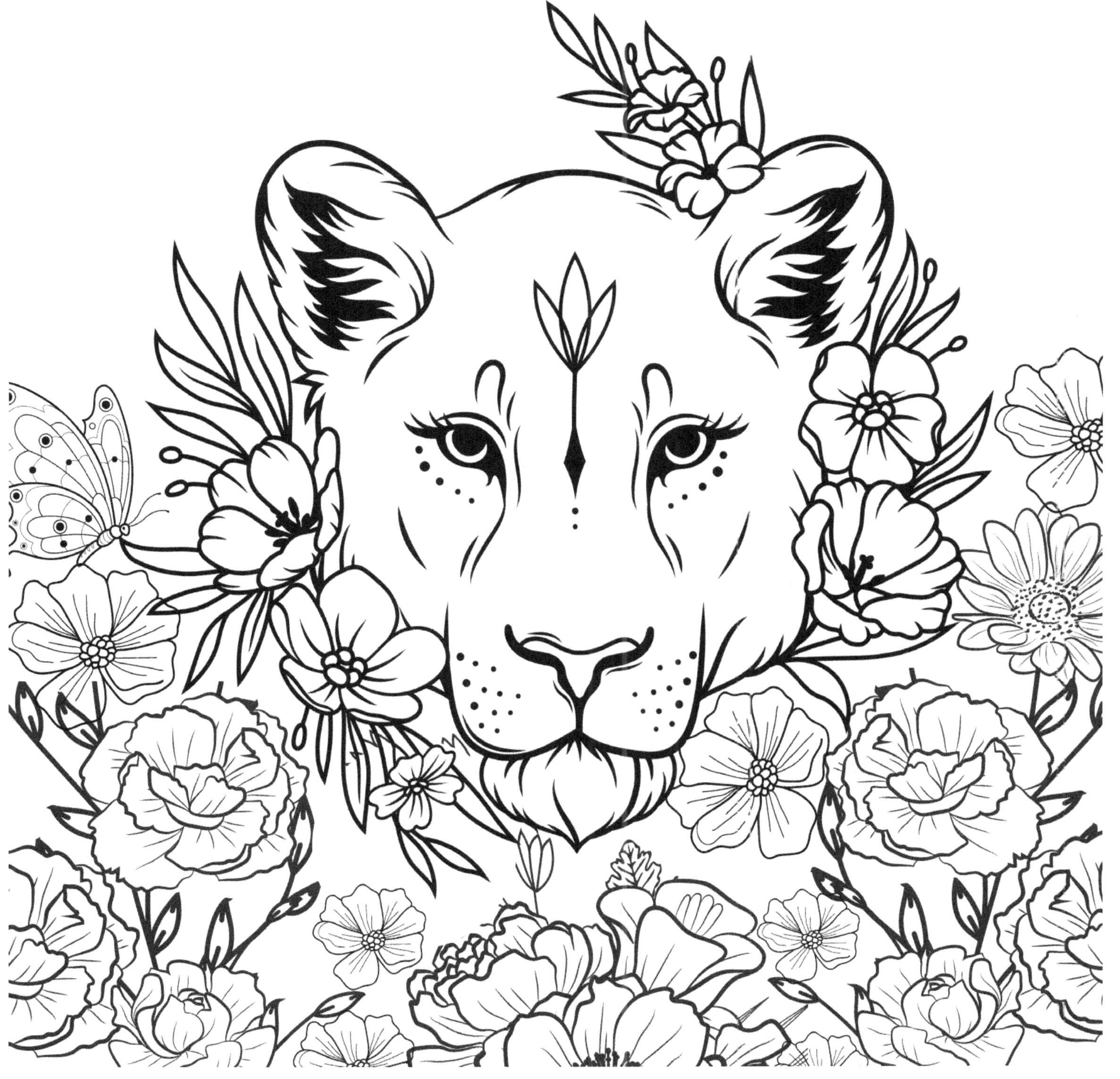

I will regain my power!

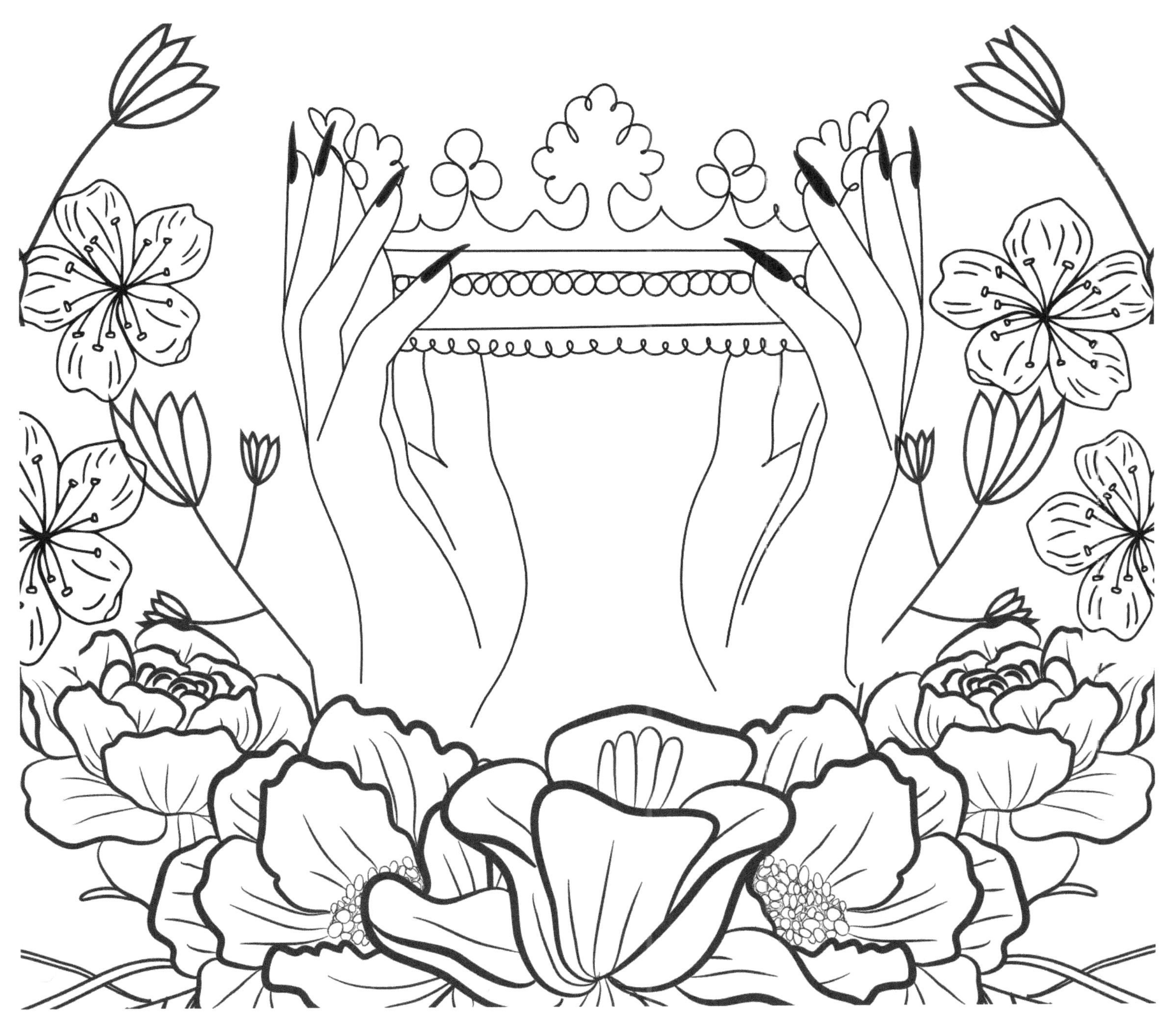

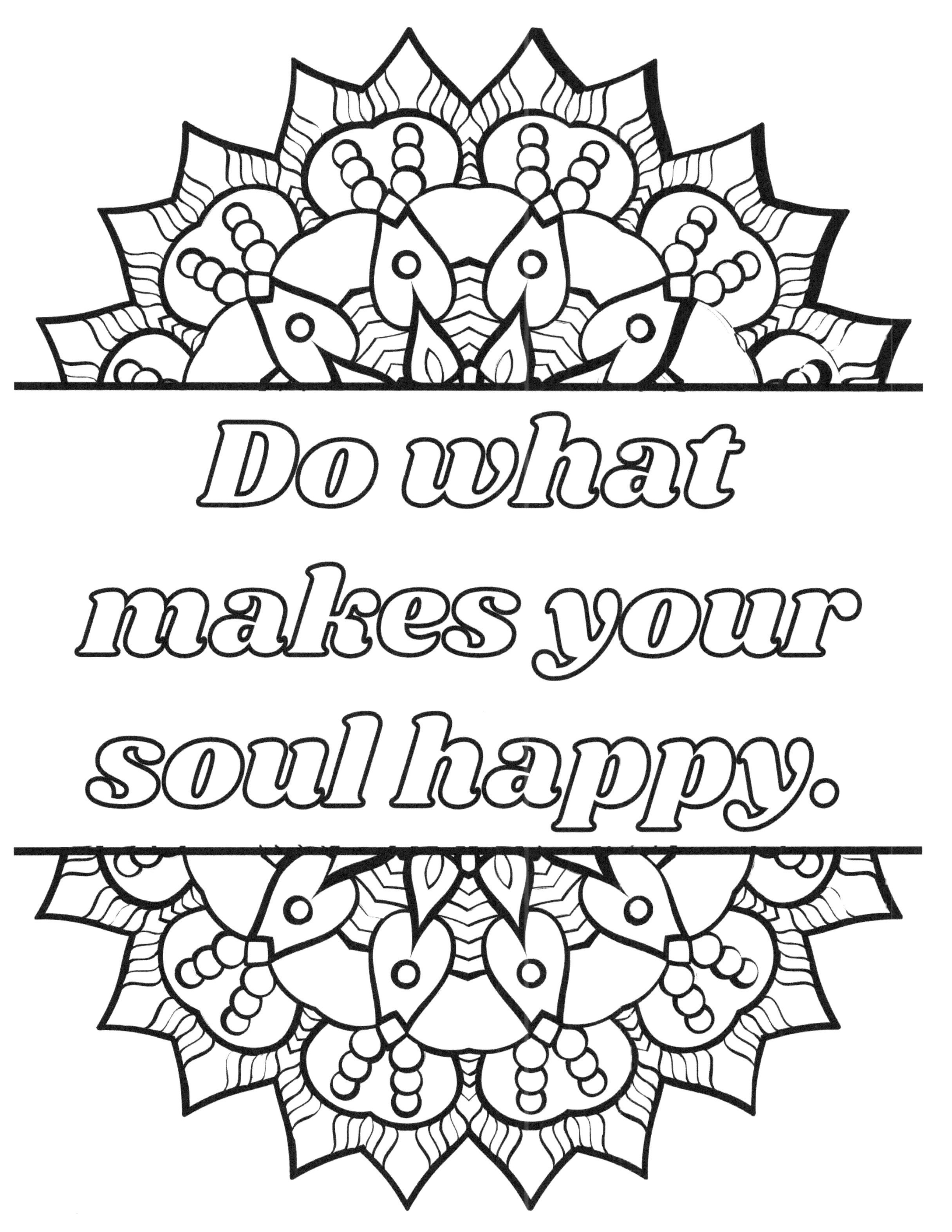
Do what
makes your
soul happy.

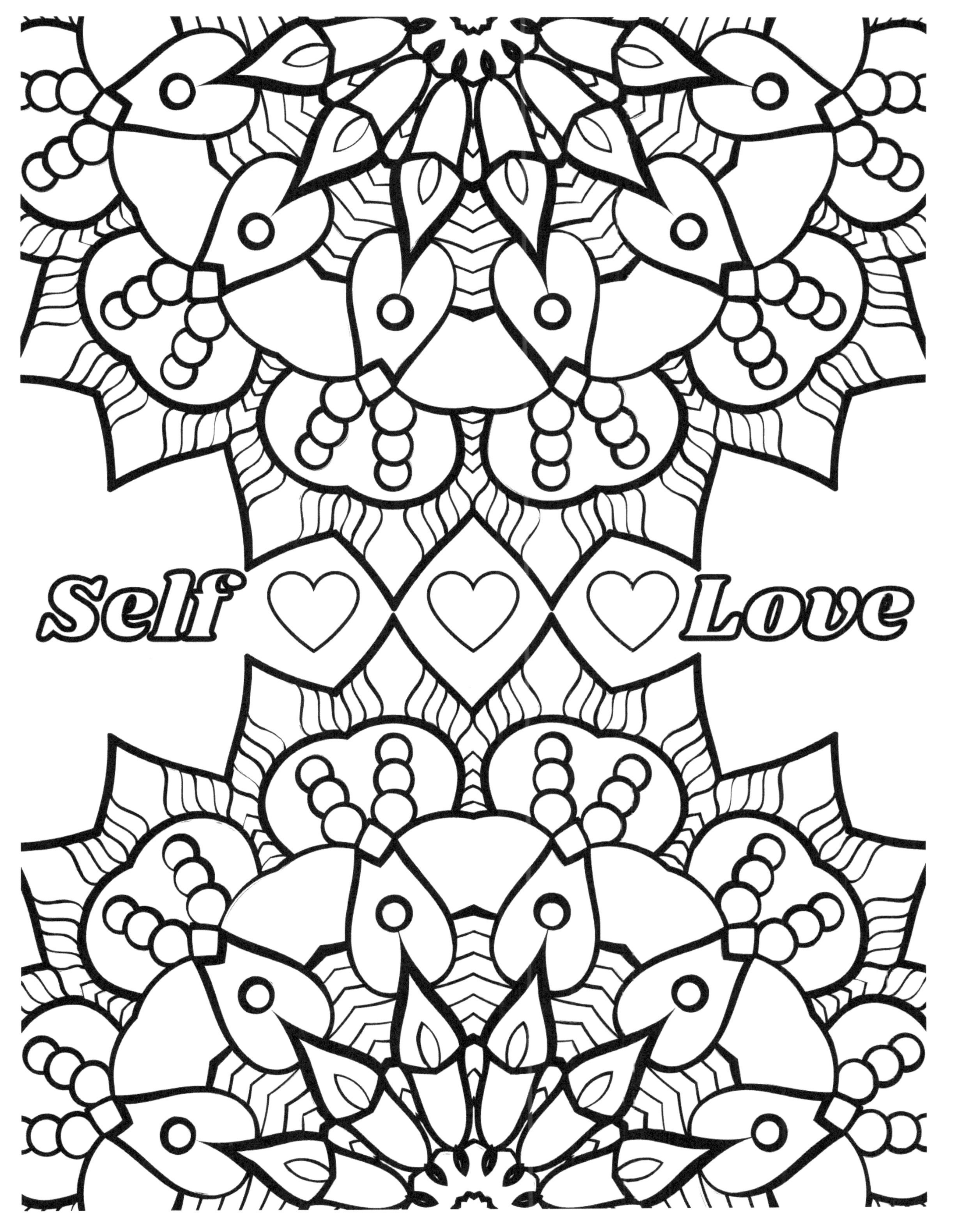
Self Love

Give yourself permission to rest.

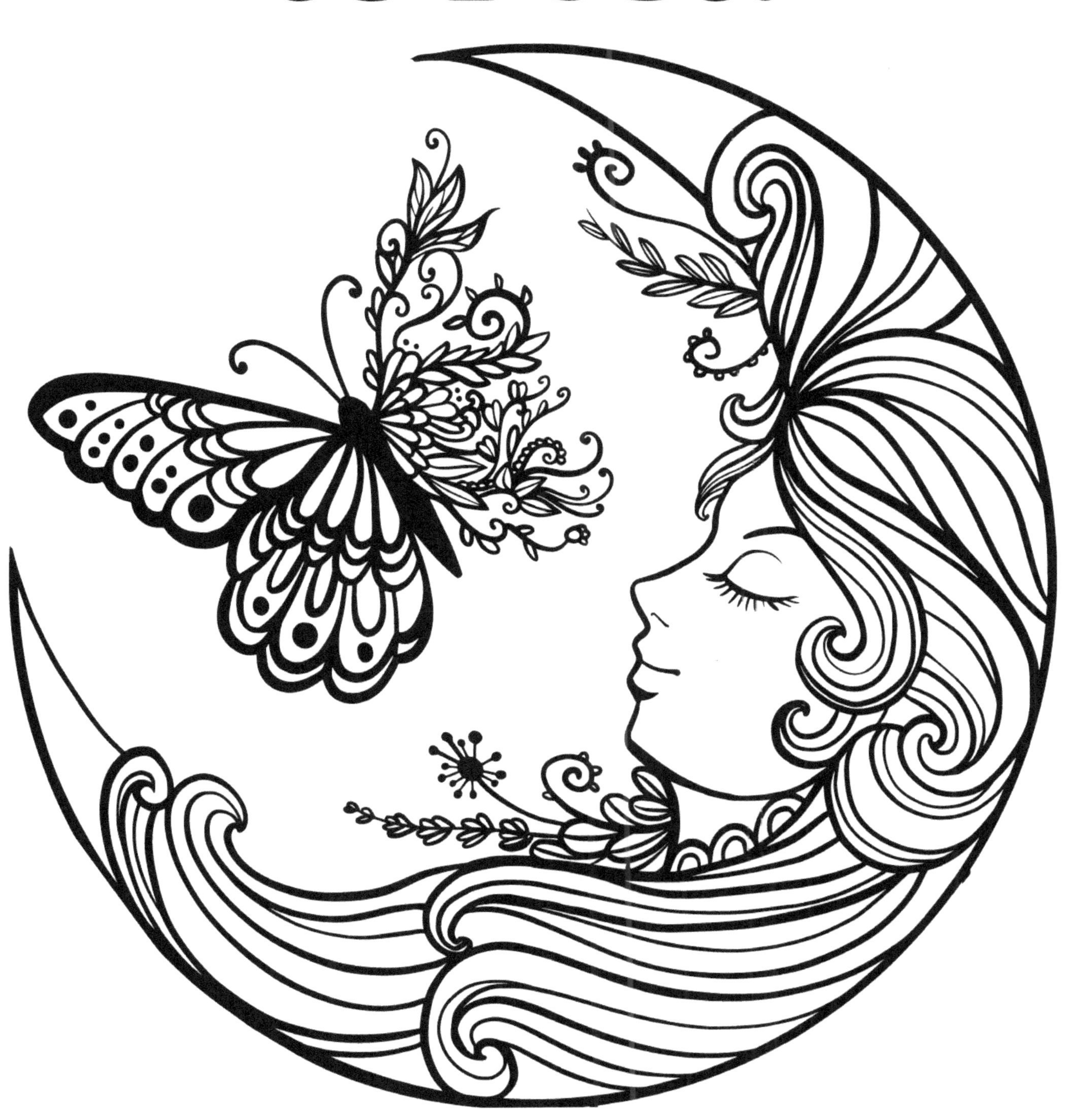

Explore the pages of your mind.

Learn when to let go.

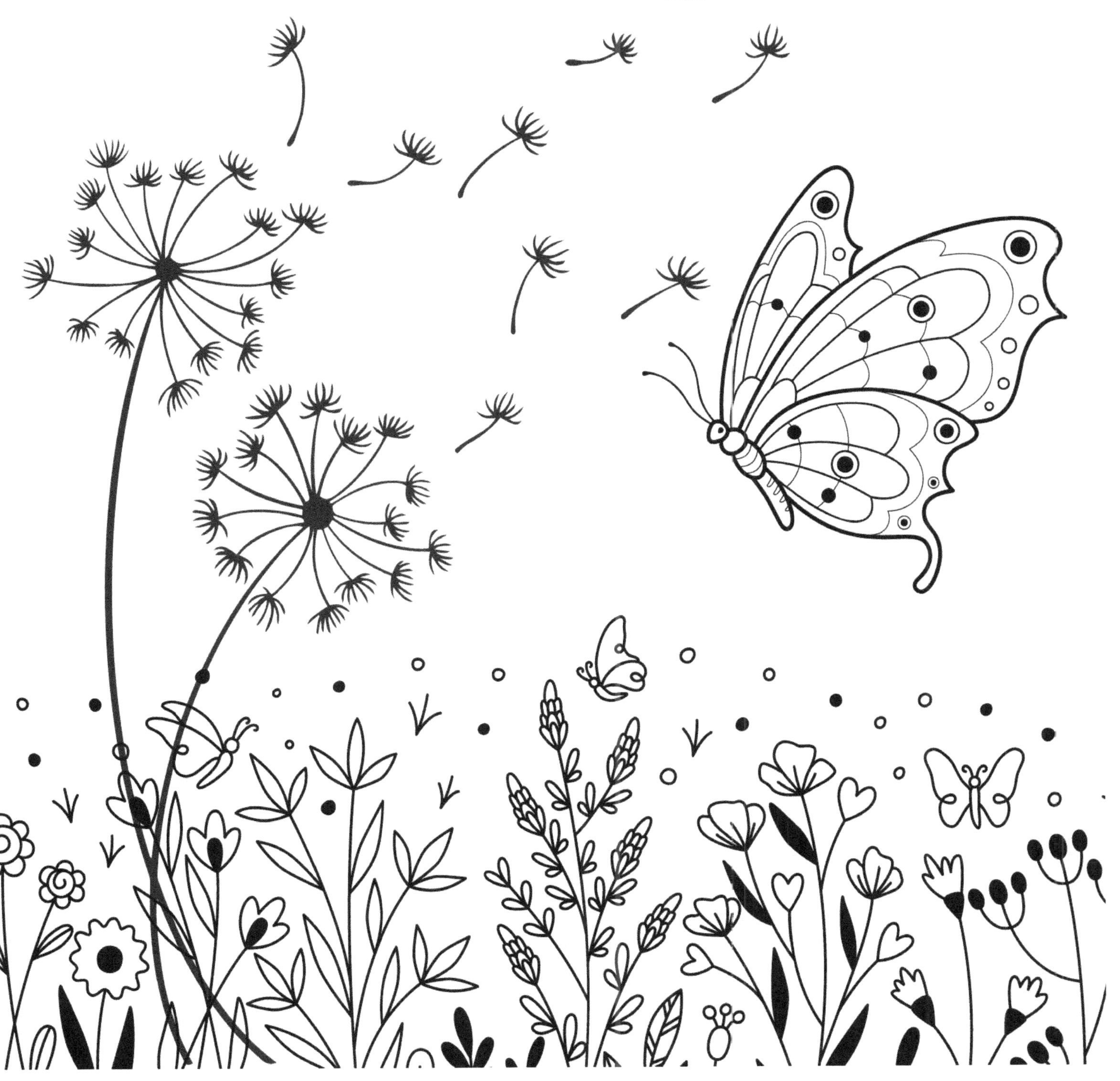

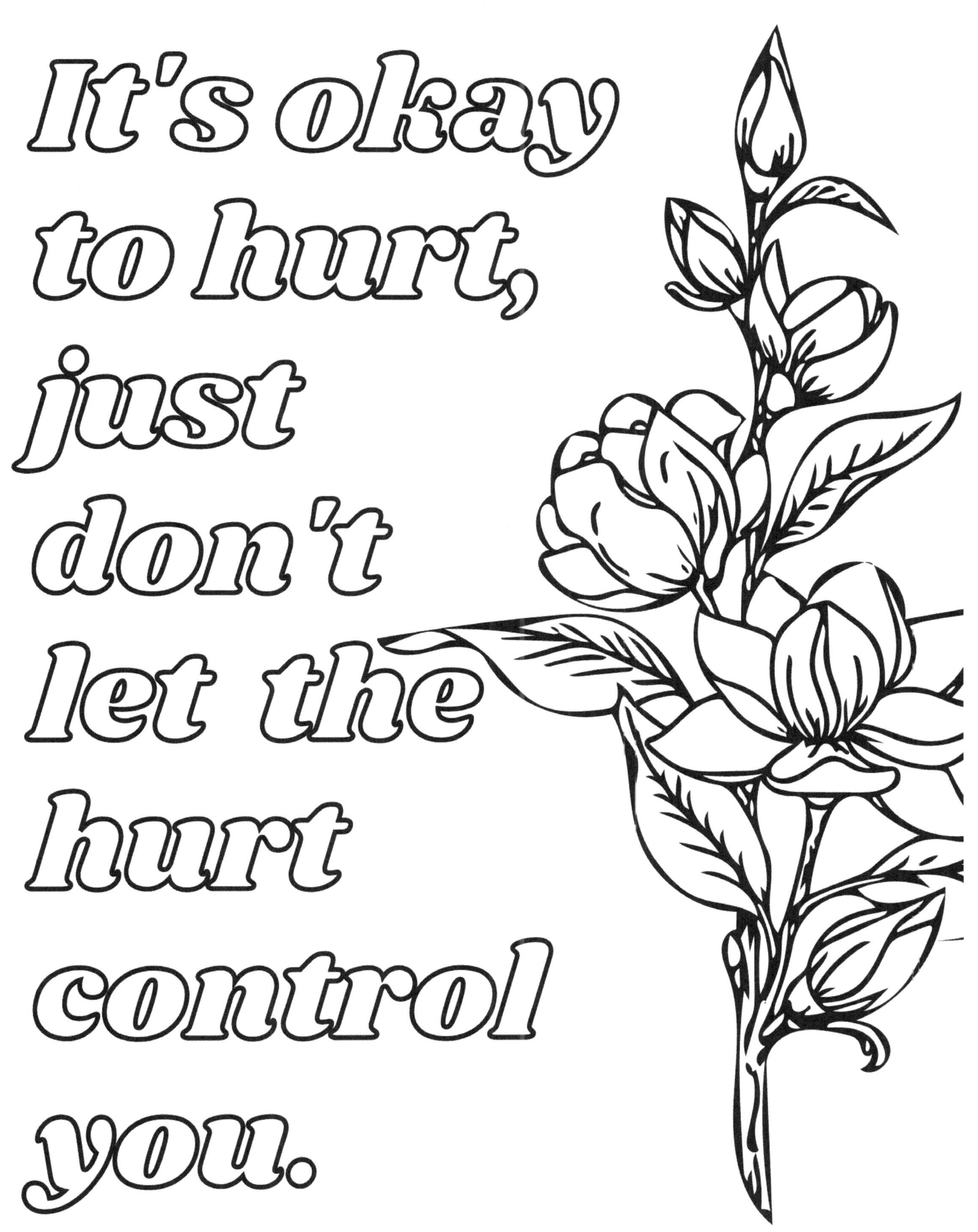
It's okay
to hurt,
just
don't
let the
hurt
control
you.

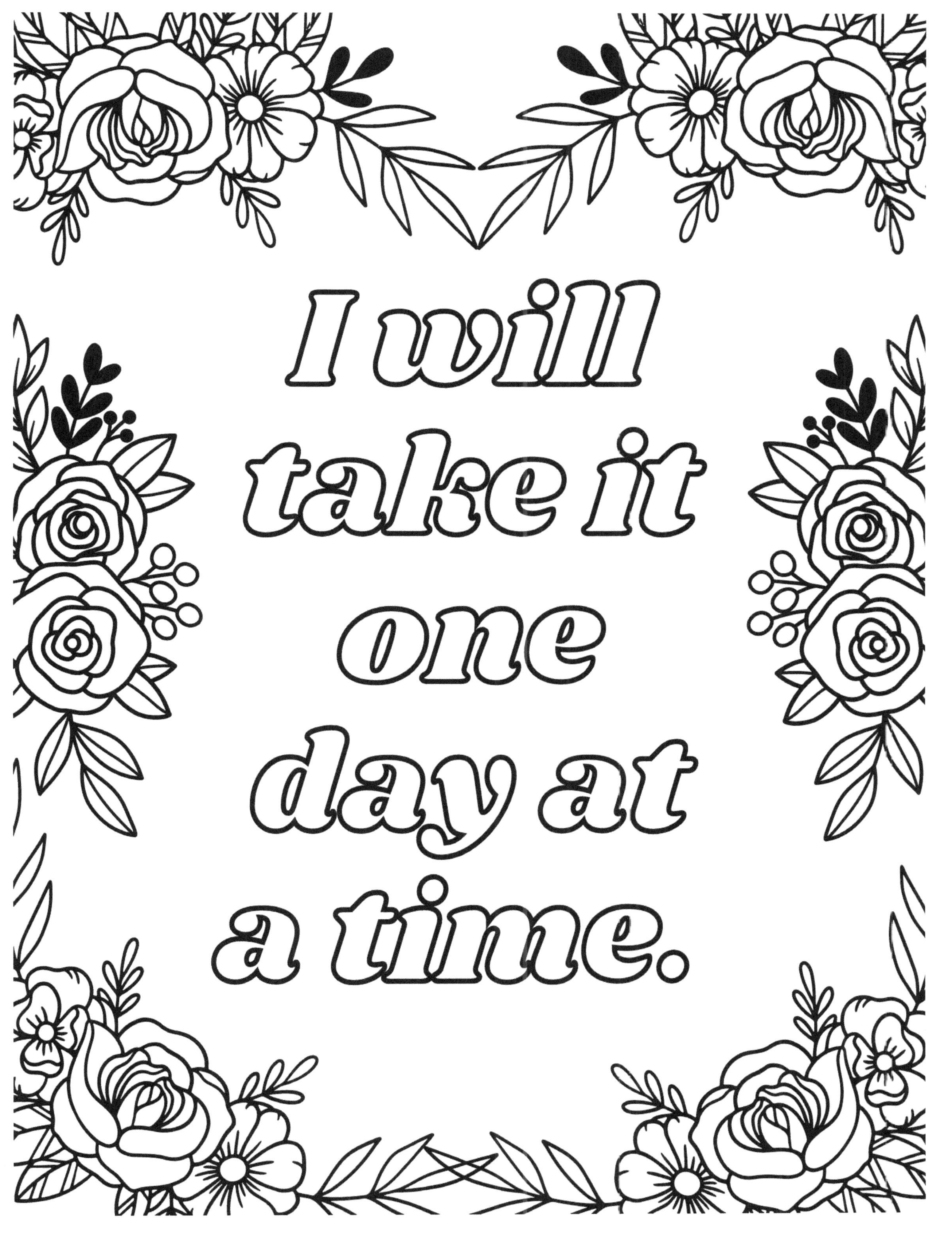
I will
take it
one
day at
a time.

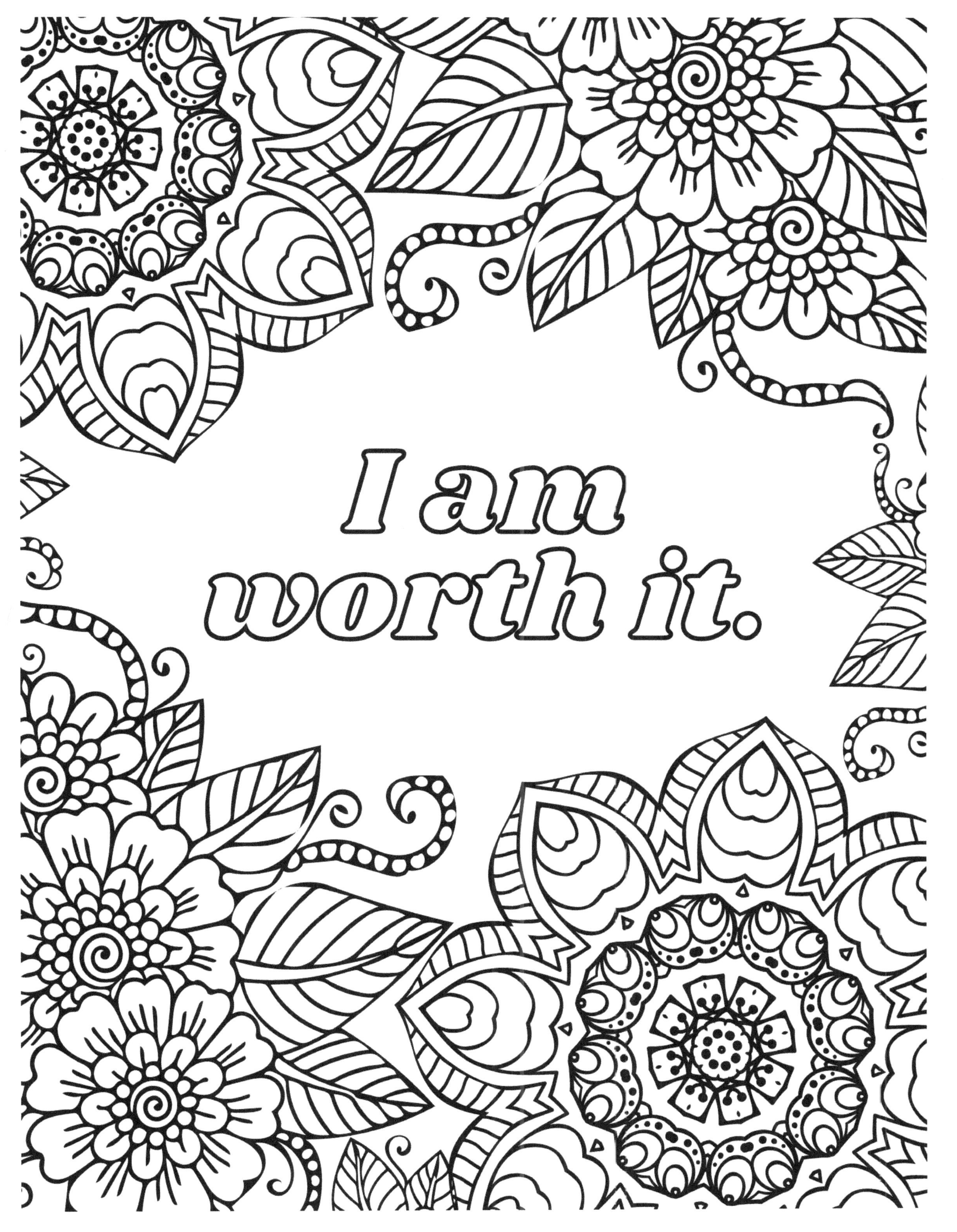
I am
worth it.

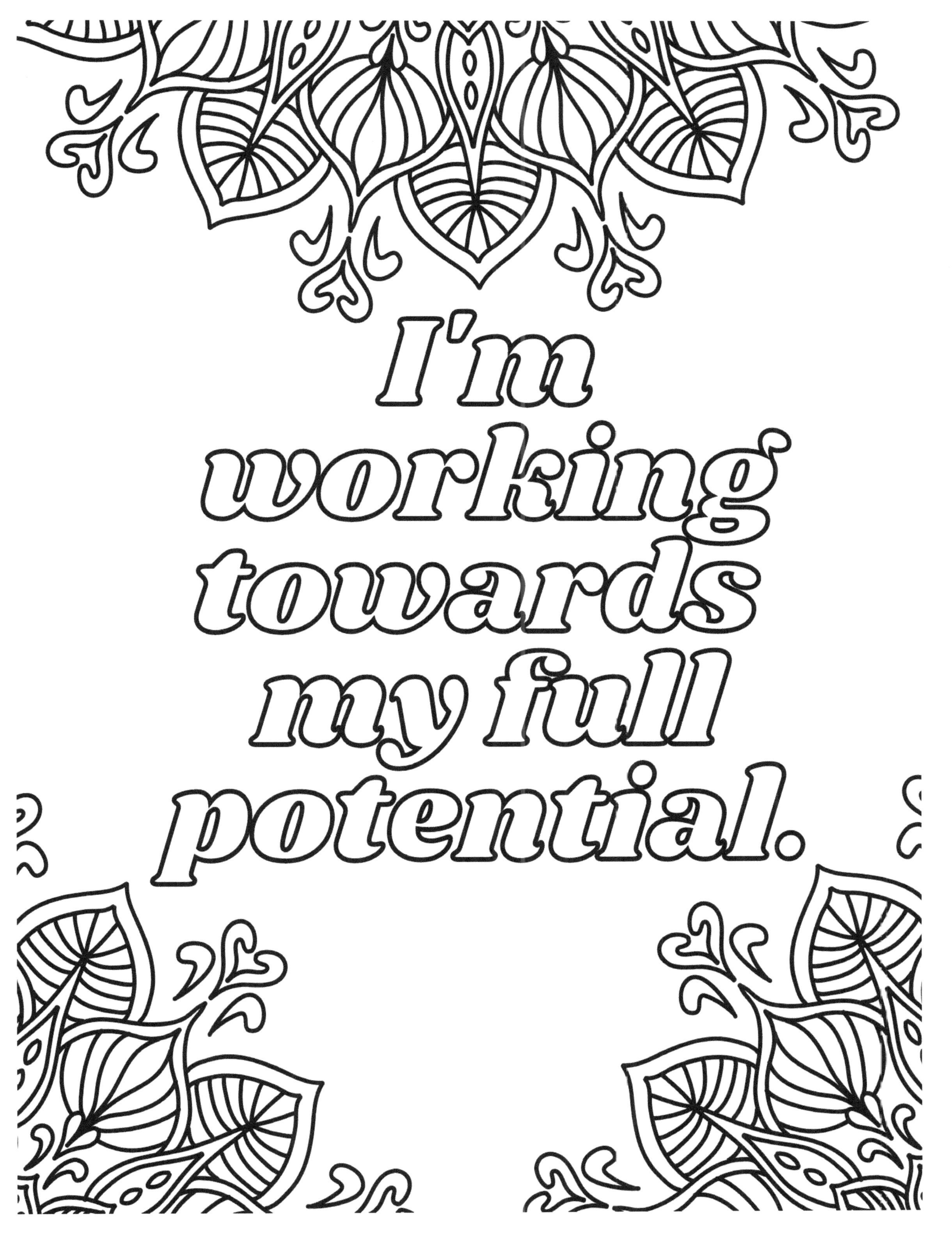
I'm working towards my full potential.

My heart

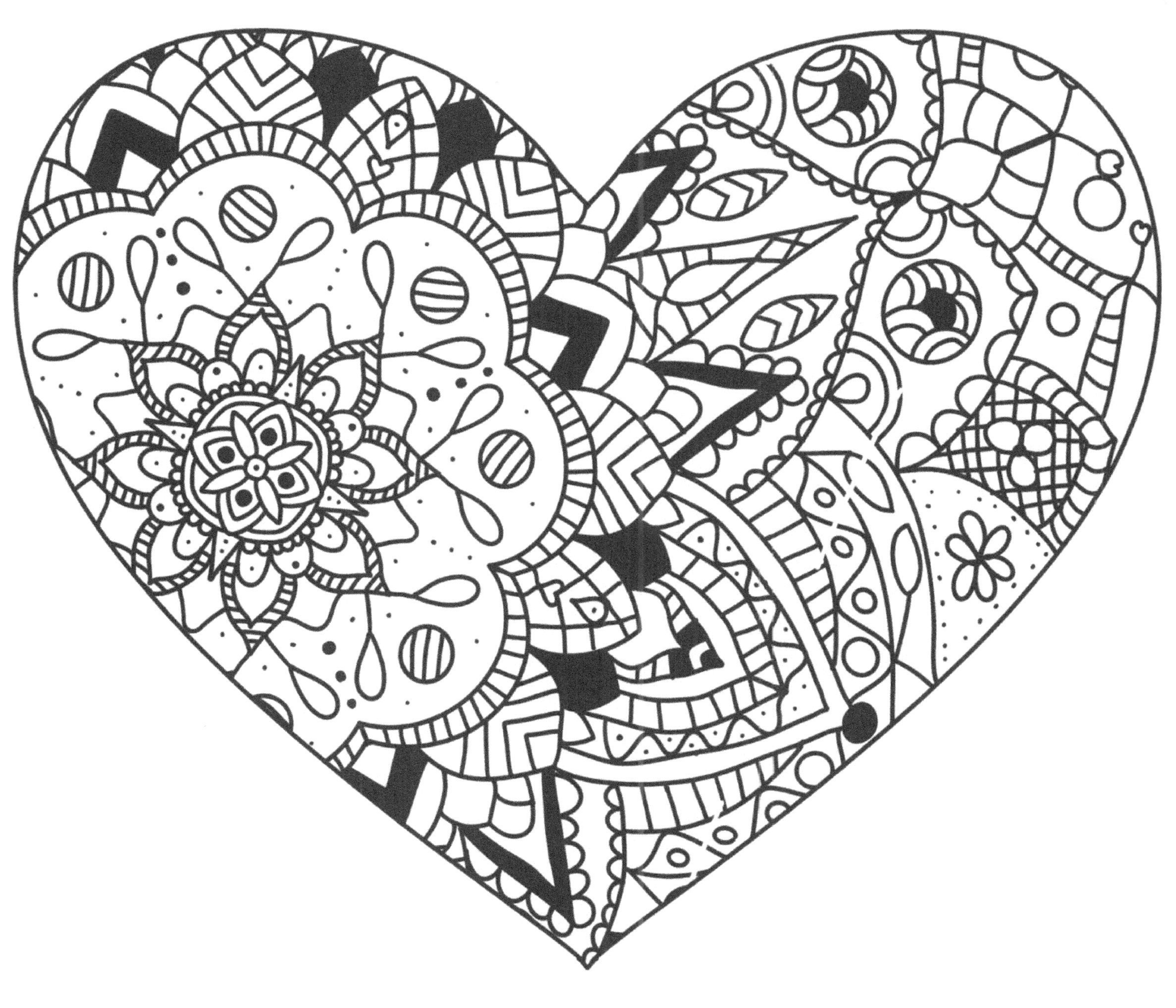

will heal.

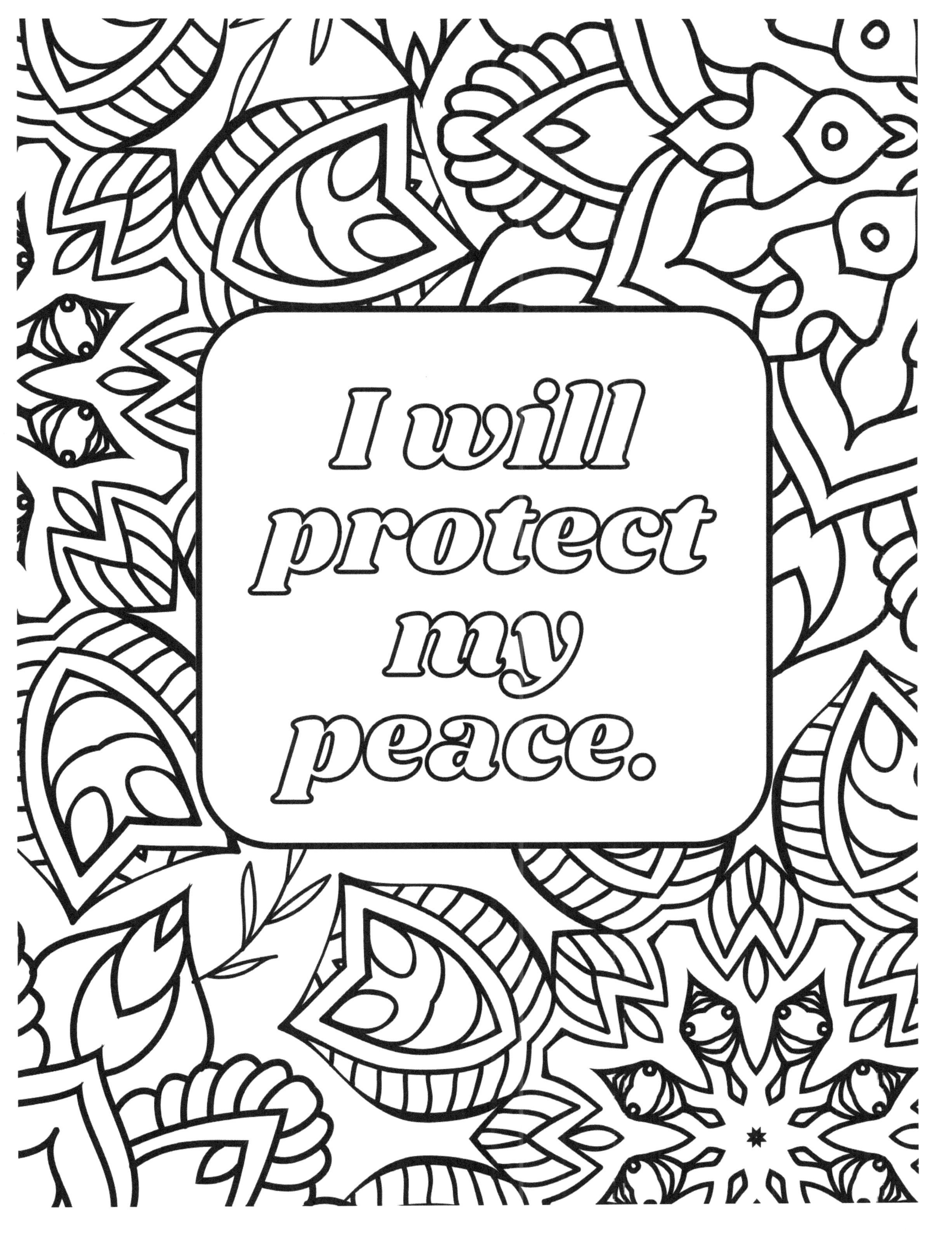
I will
protect
my
peace.

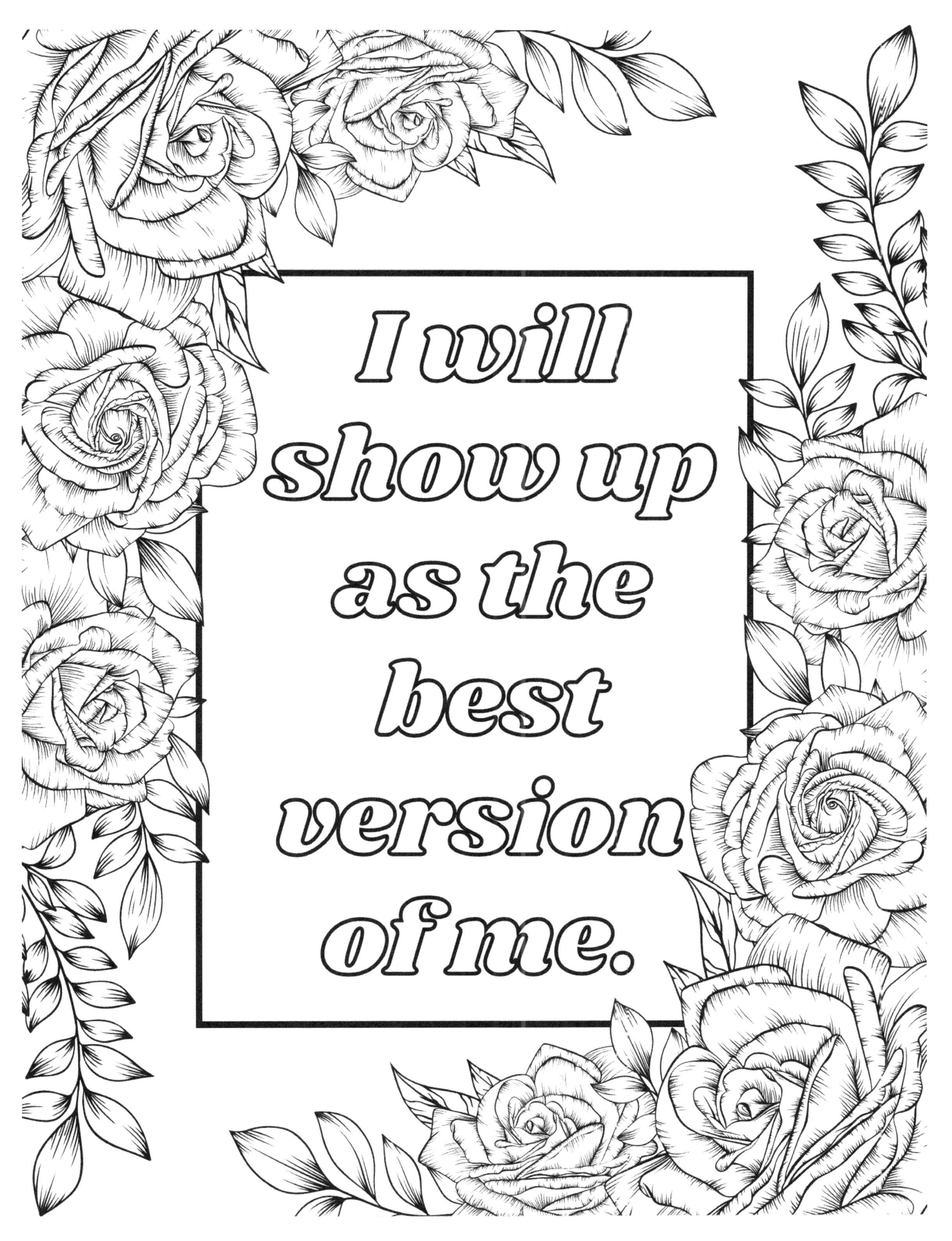
I will
show up
as the
best
version
of me.

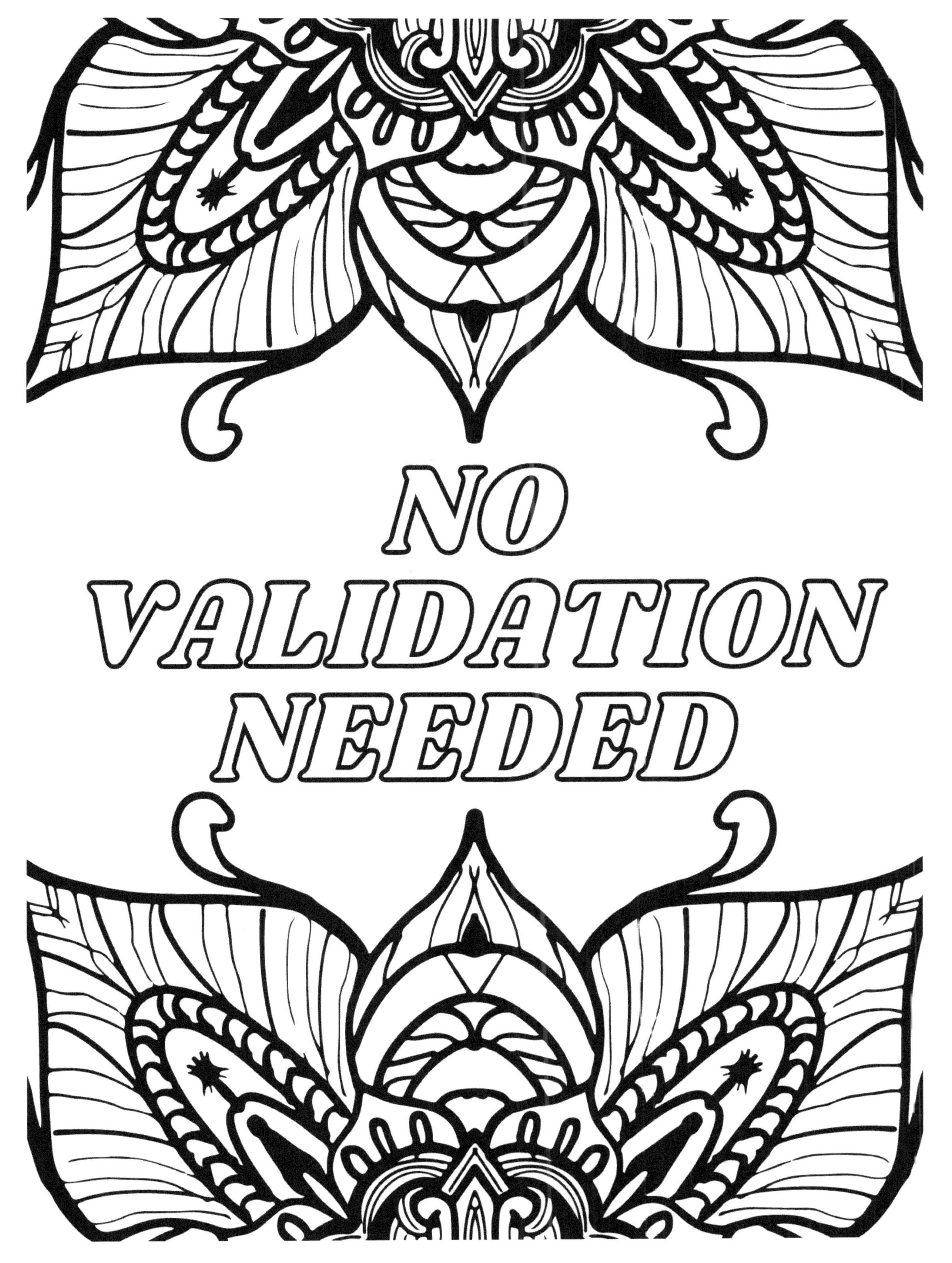
NO
VALIDATION
NEEDED

I am beautiful.

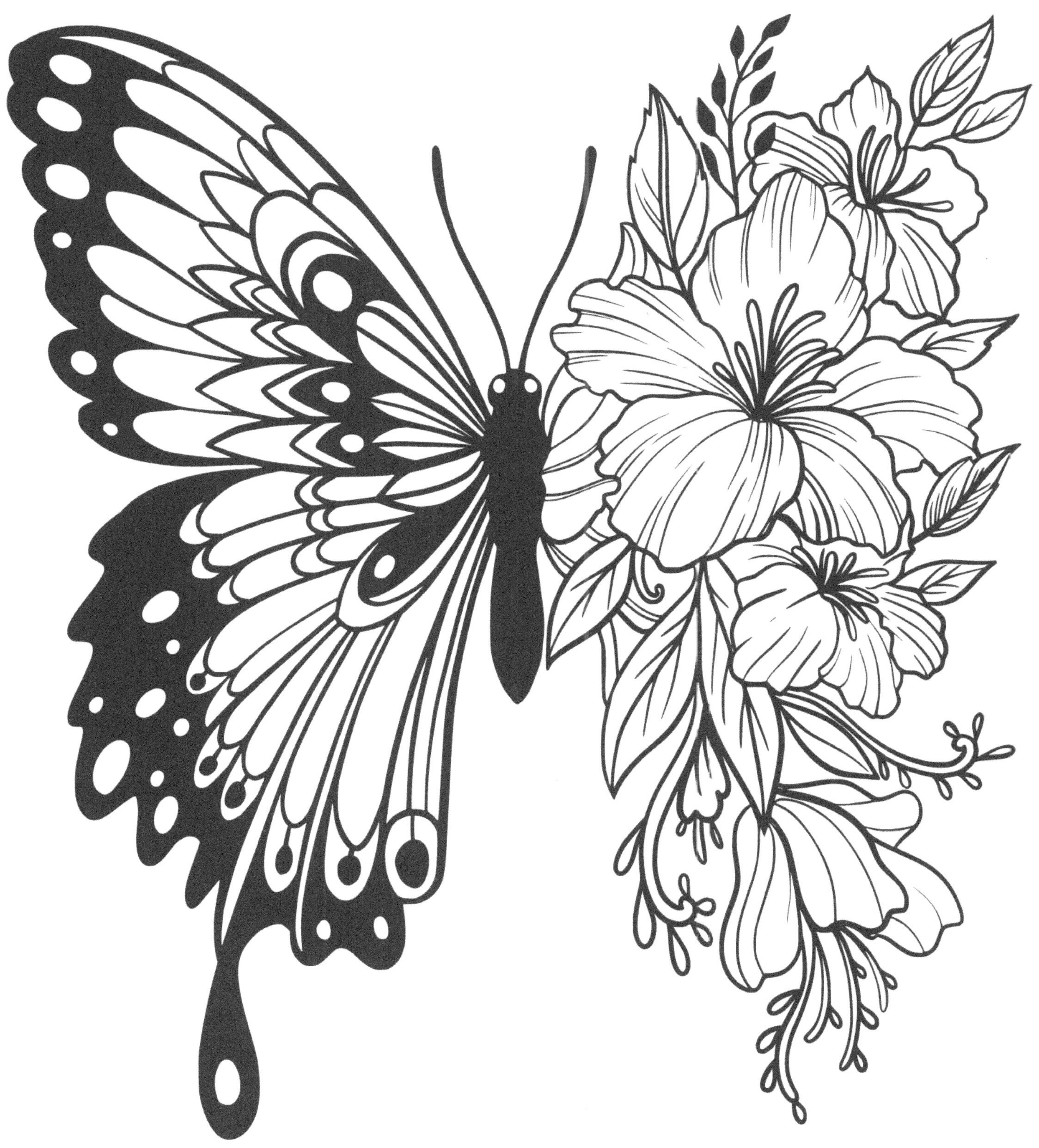

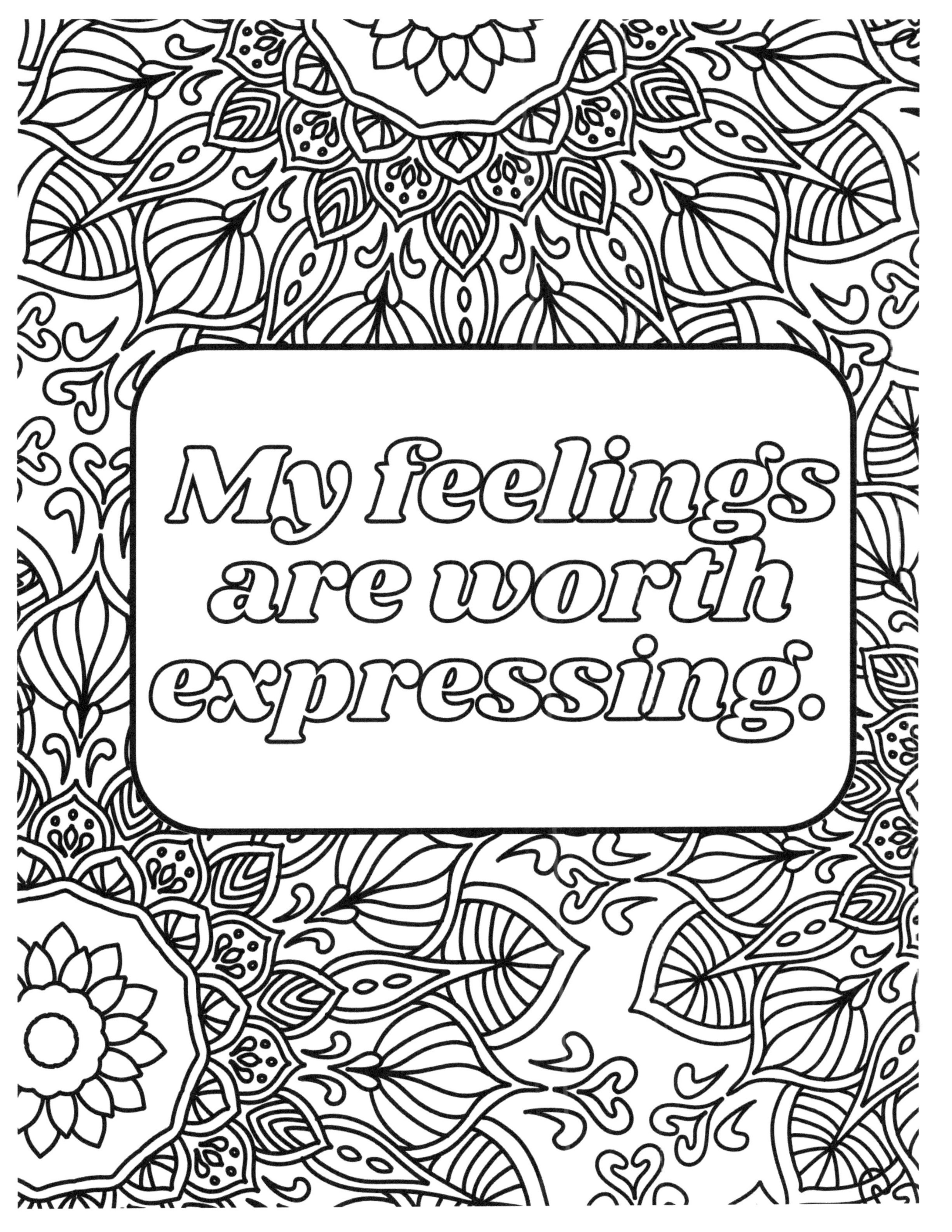
My feelings are worth expressing.

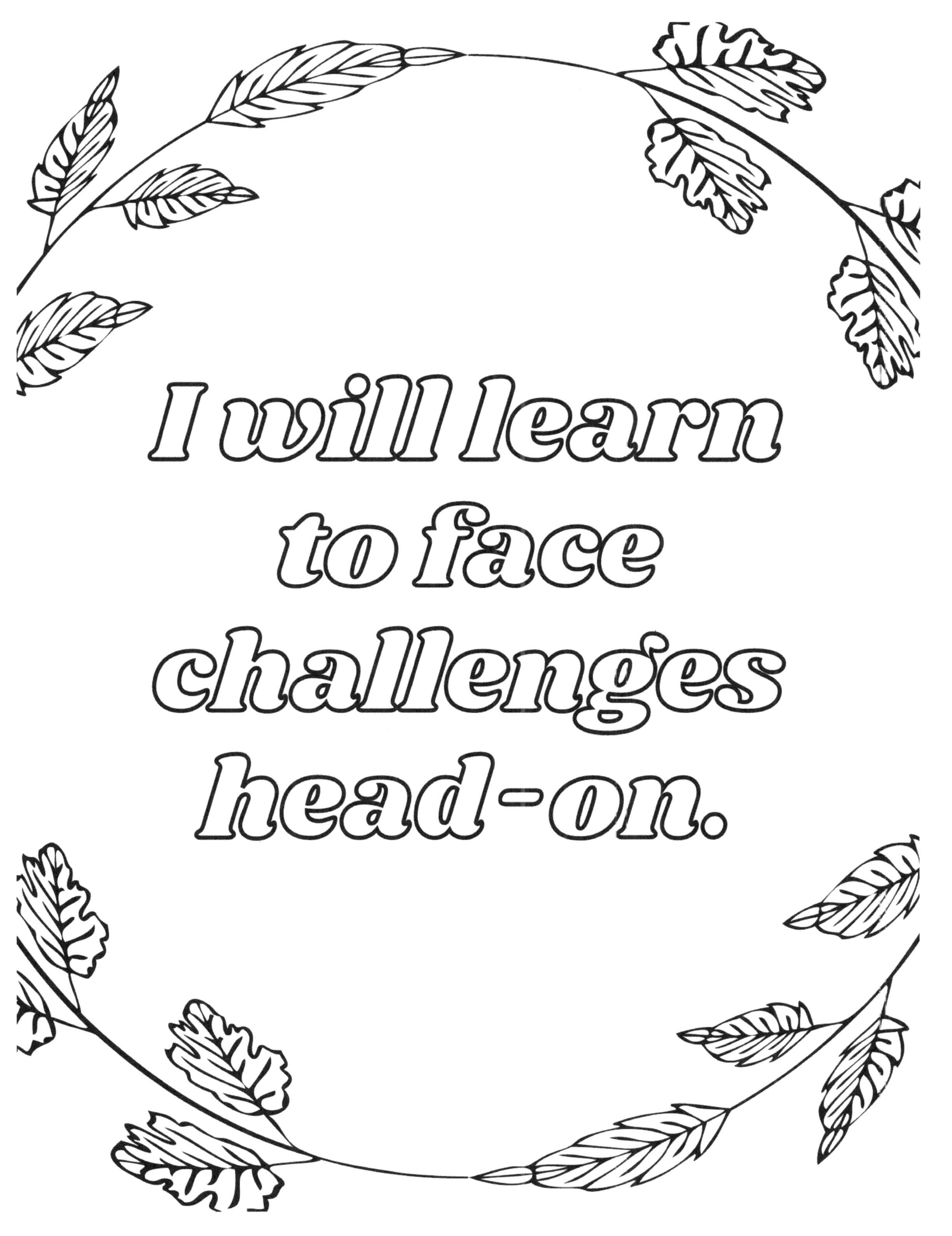
I will learn
to face
challenges
head-on.

I won't
waste a
single
moment.

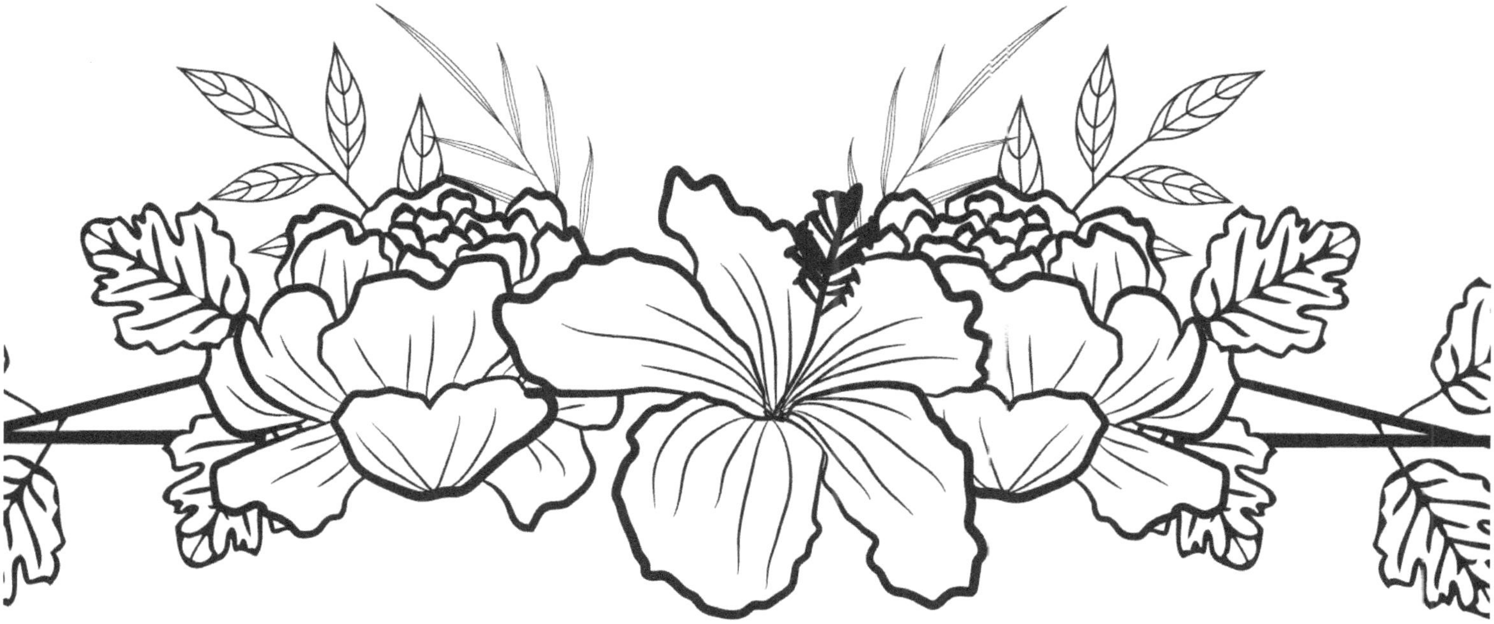

I deserve EVERYTHING that life has to offer.

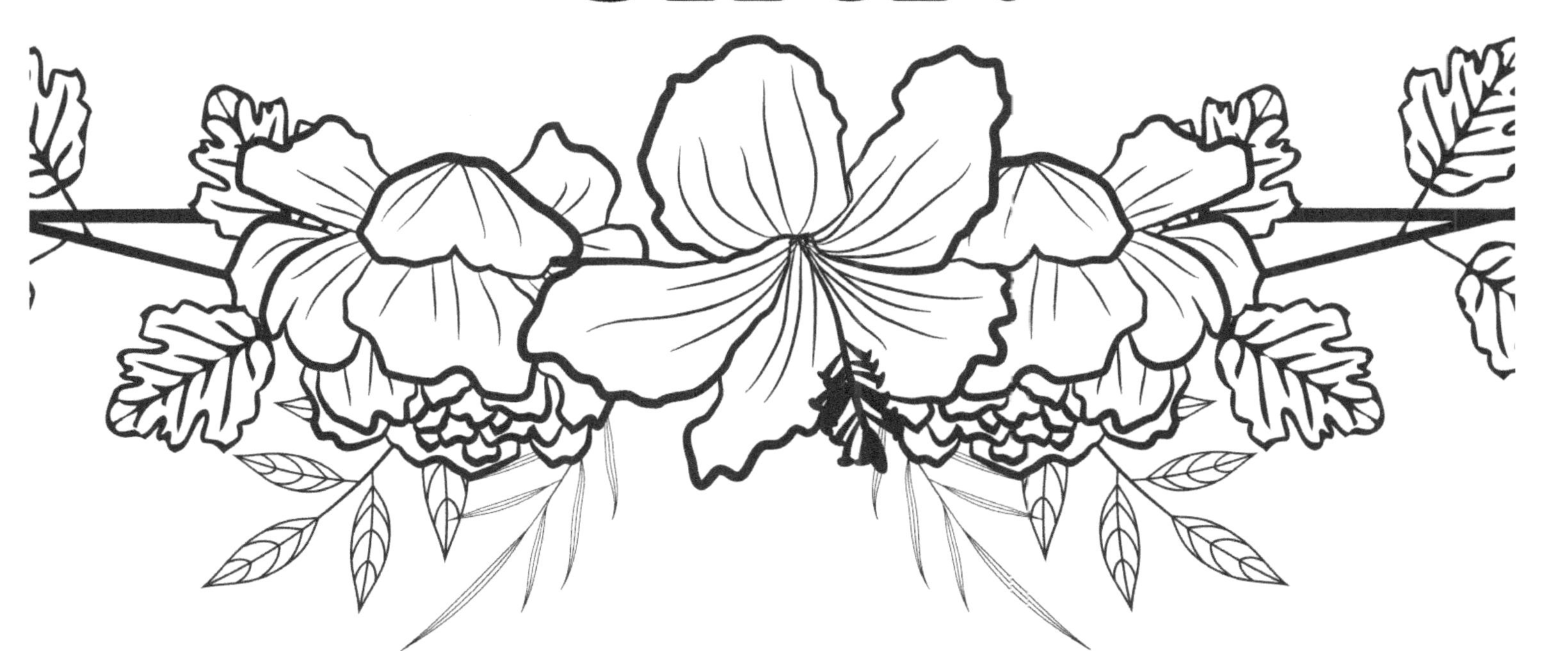

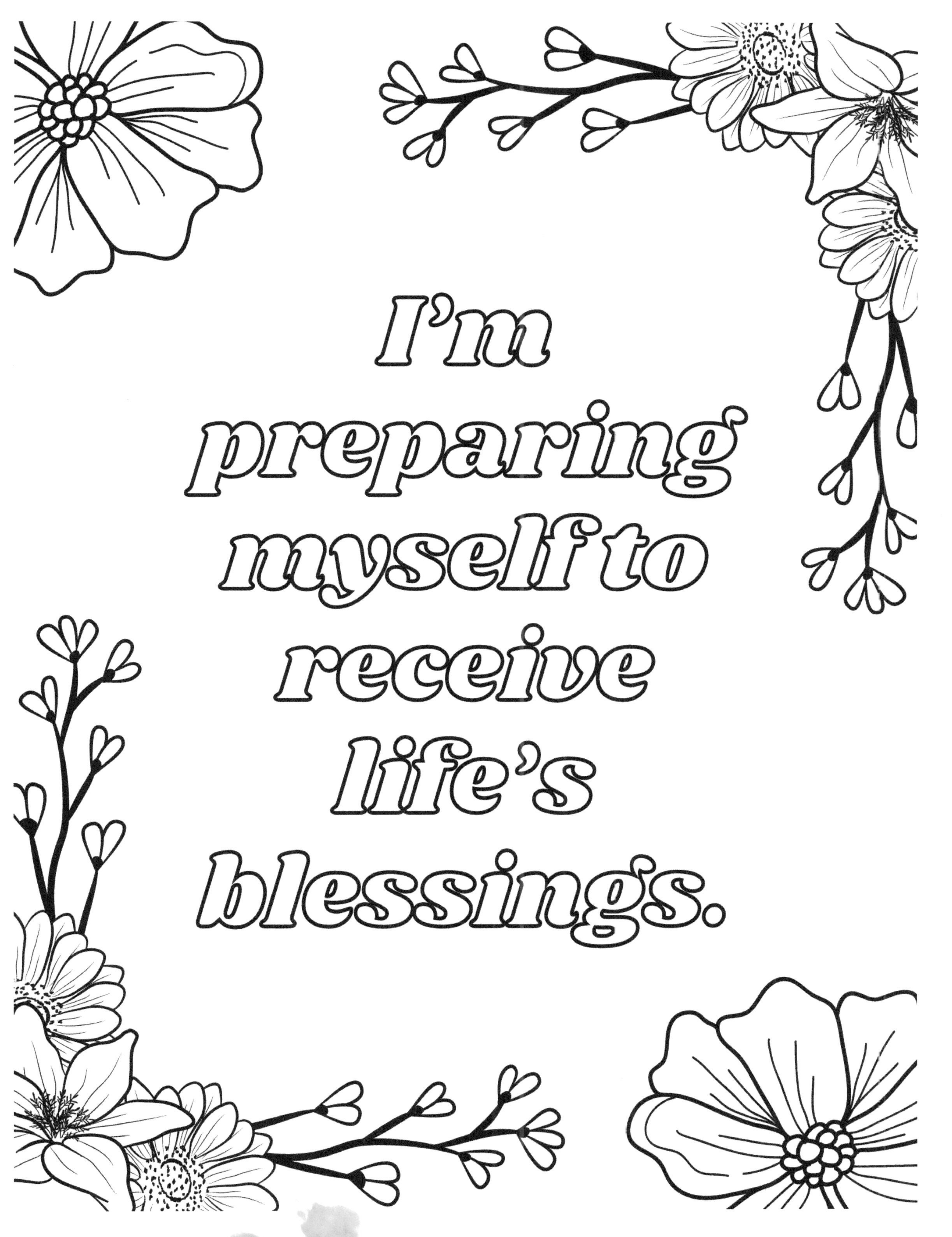
I'm
preparing
myself to
receive
life's
blessings.

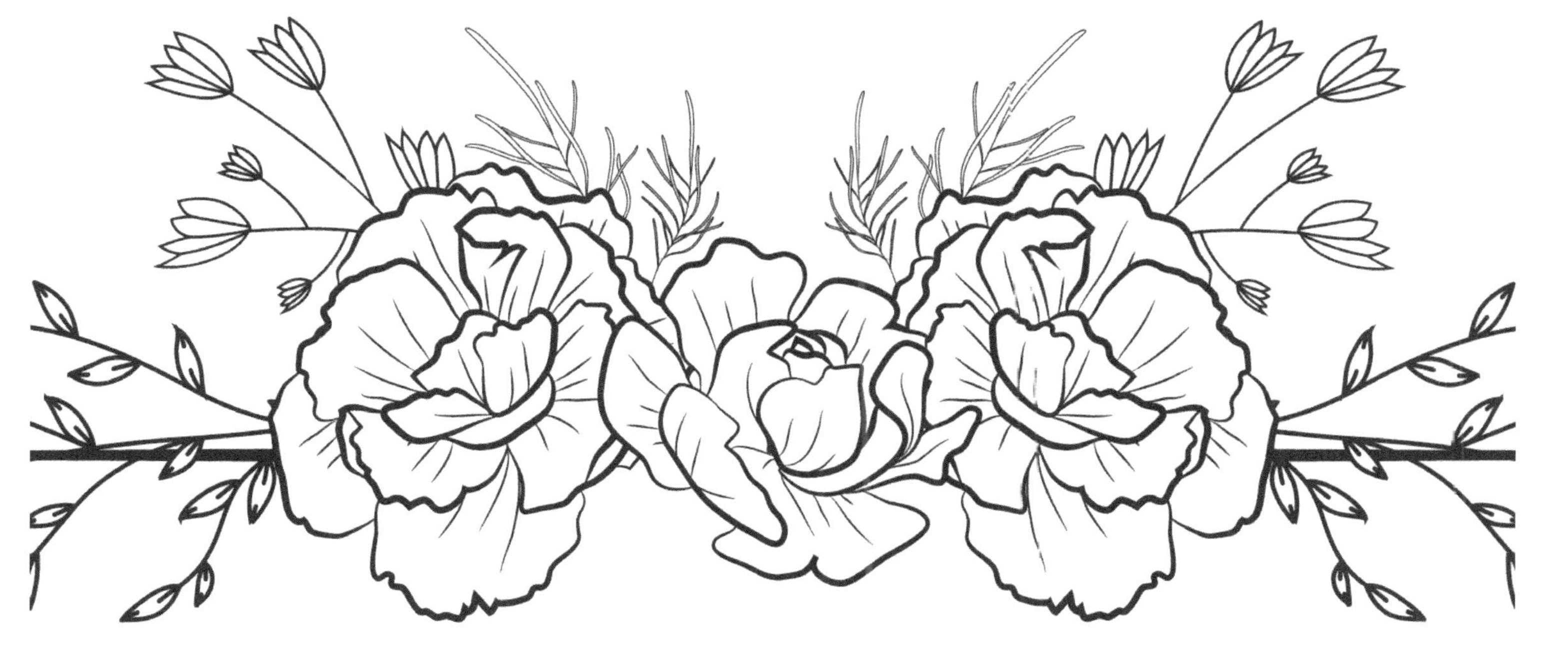

I emit radiance, positivity, and wholeness.

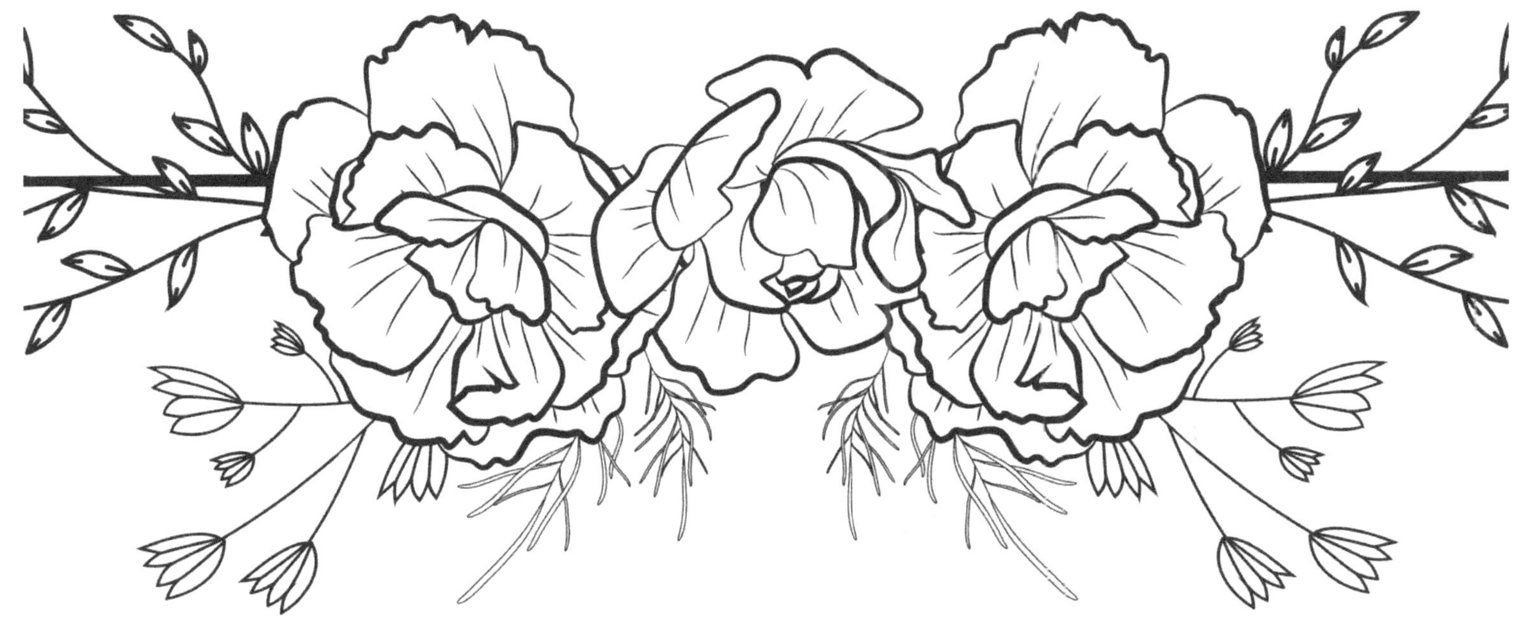

It's time to spread my wings!

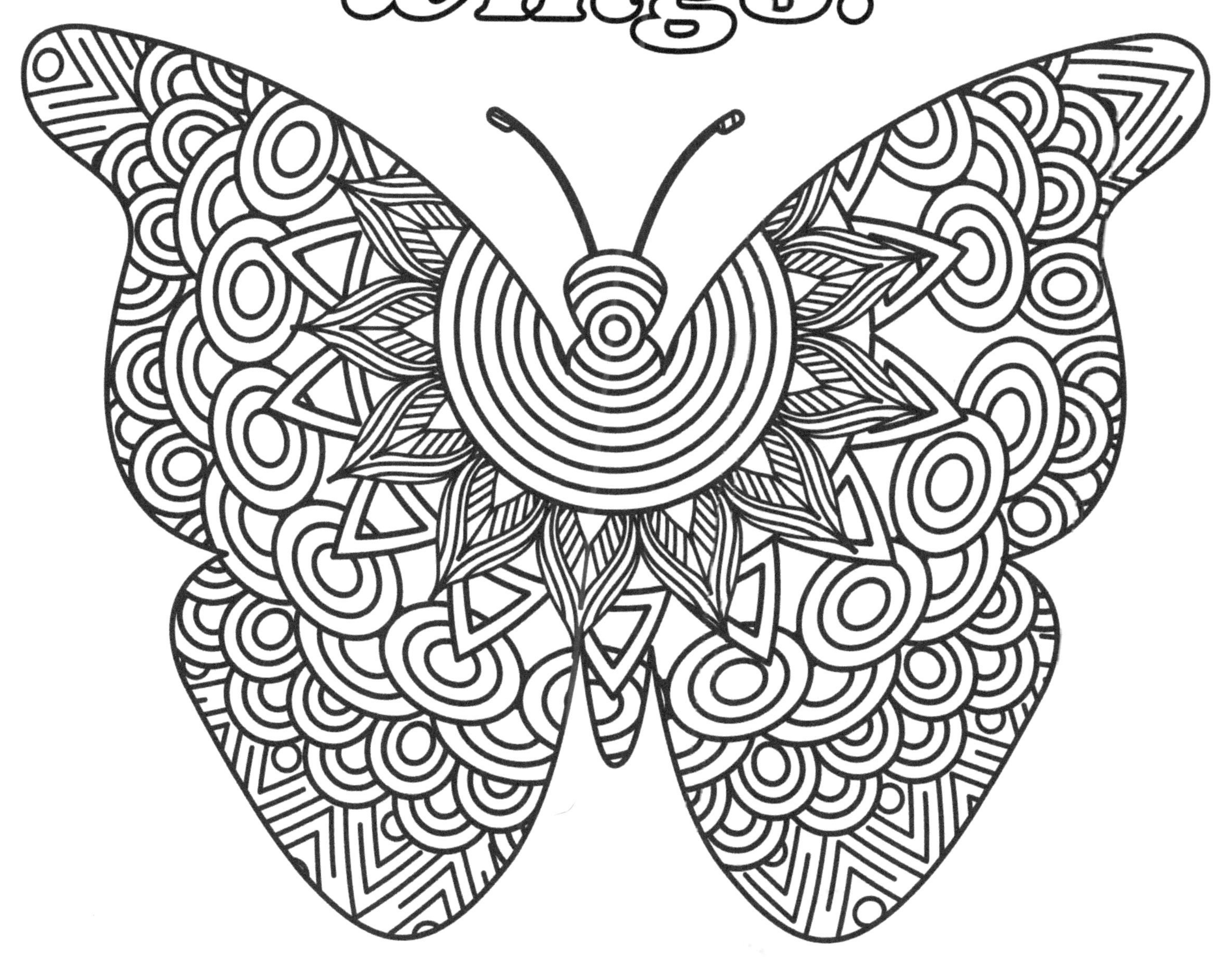

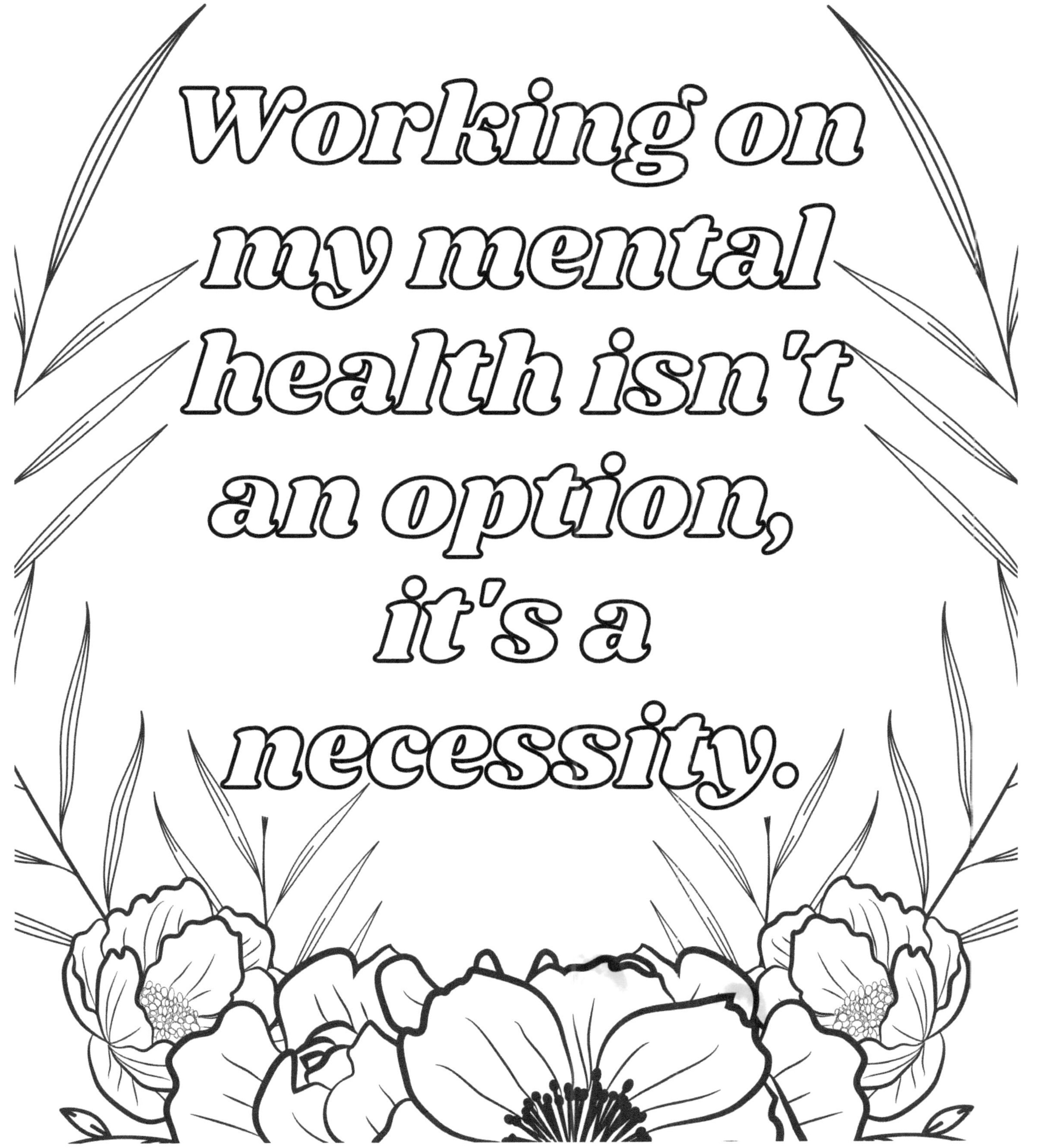
Working on
my mental
health isn't
an option,
it's a
necessity.

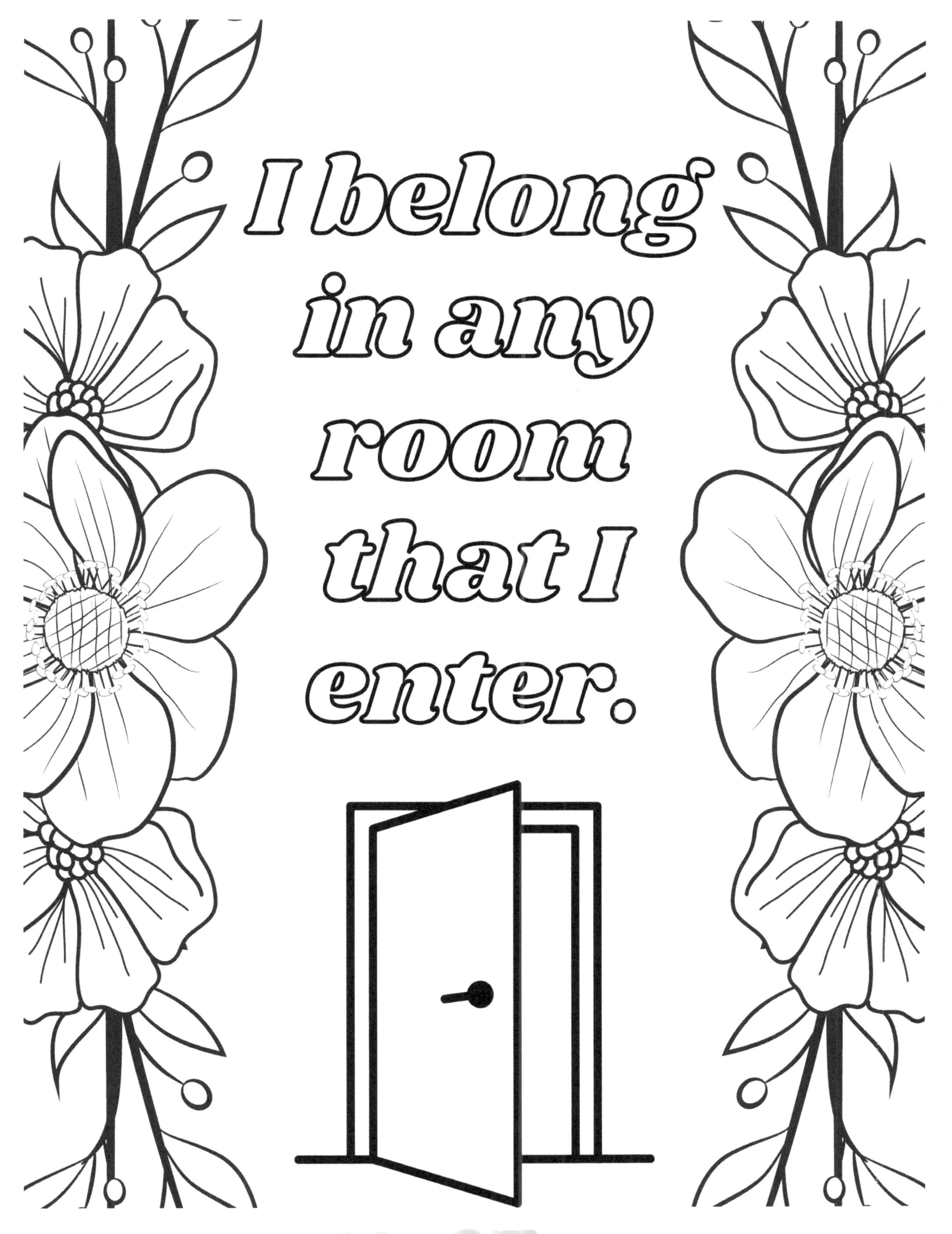
I belong
in any
room
that I
enter.

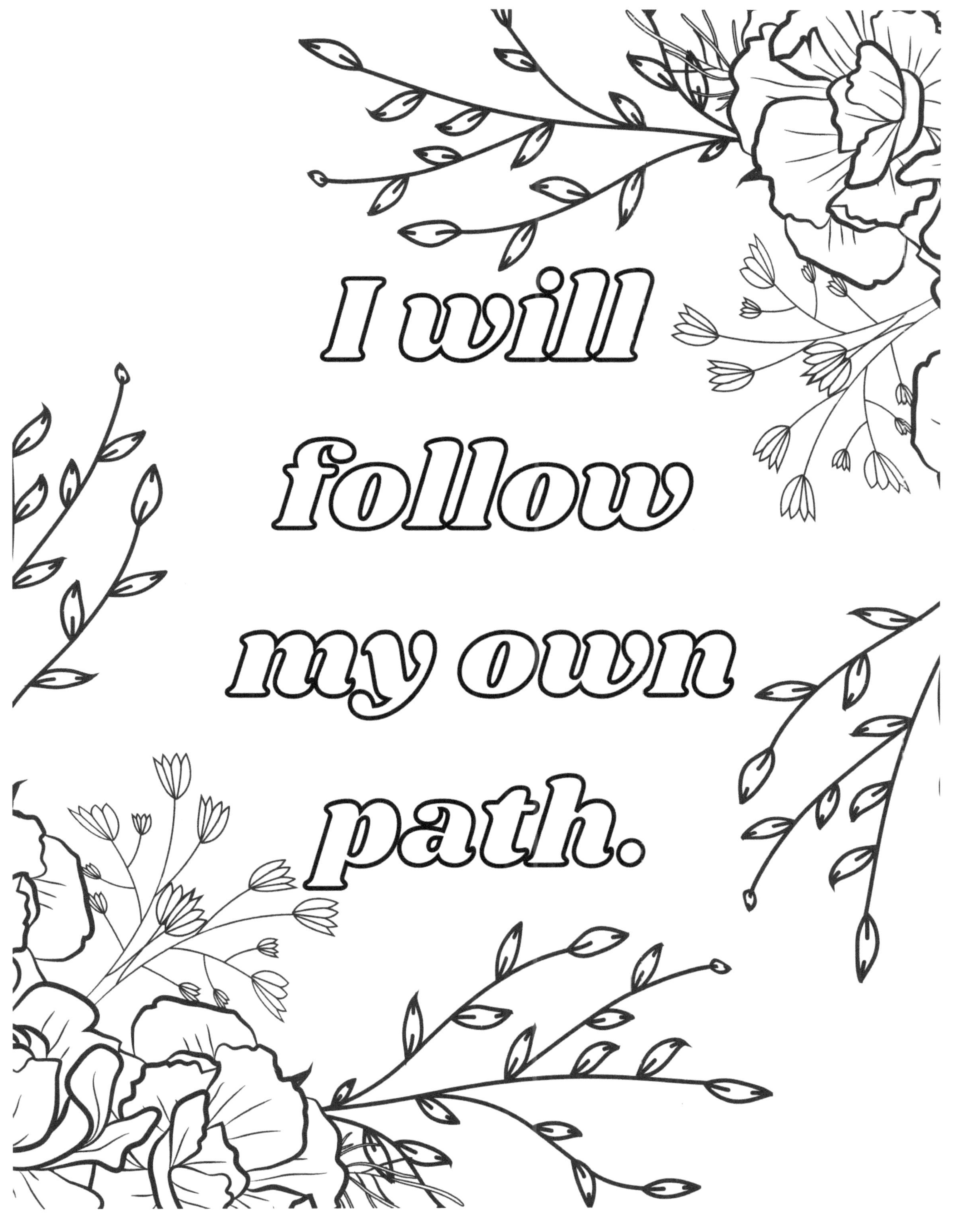
I will
follow
my own
path.

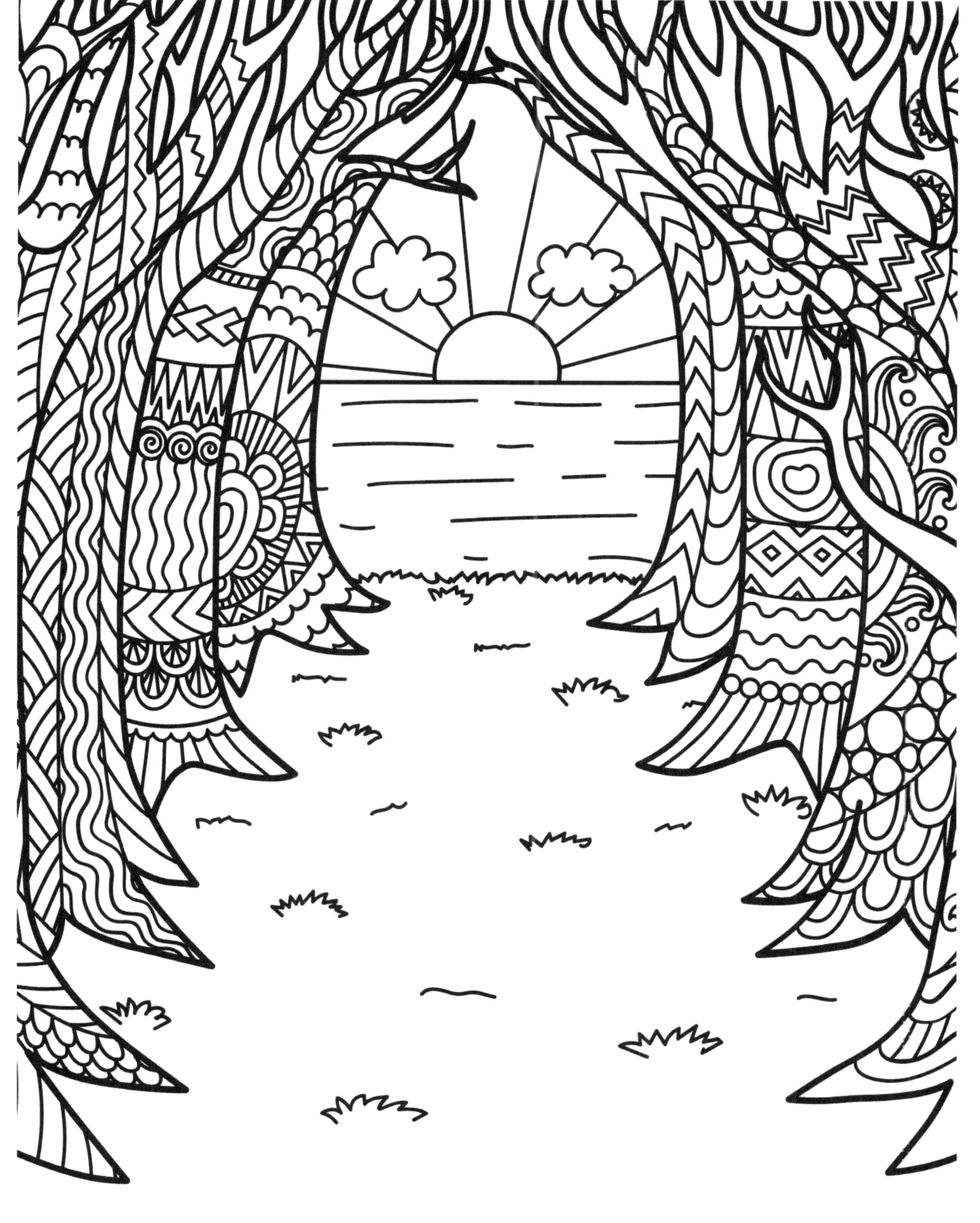

www.ingramcontent.com/pod-product-compliance
Lightning Source LLC
LaVergne TN
LVHW081418110826
845149LV00010B/1787

* 9 7 8 1 9 5 5 7 2 7 3 6 5 *